MATH TRAILBLAZERS™

Grade 4

Unit Resource Guide
Unit 3

Numbers and Number Operations

SECOND EDITION

A Mathematical Journey Using Science and Language Arts

KENDALL/HUNT PUBLISHING COMPANY
4050 Westmark Drive   Dubuque, Iowa 52002

A TIMS® Curriculum
University of Illinois at Chicago

UIC The University of Illinois
at Chicago

The original edition was based on work supported by the National Science Foundation under grant
No. MDR 9050226 and the University of Illinois at Chicago. Any opinions, findings, and conclusions
or recommendations expressed in this publication are those of the author(s) and do not necessarily
reflect the views of the granting agencies.

LETTER HOME

Numbers and Number Operations

Date: _____

Dear Family Member:

In this unit we focus on strengthening your child's understanding of our number system, including place value and negative numbers. To be able to compute, we need to understand place value: the idea that the value of a digit in a number depends upon where it is placed. For example, the 2 in 426 is 2 tens but in 4235 it is 2 hundreds. This unit reviews addition and subtraction with an emphasis on understanding place value. Students use estimation to check the reasonableness of their answers.

We also begin a review of the multiplication facts and a systematic study of the division facts. Your child should know all the basic math facts by the end of the school year.

Help your child learn about place value, negative numbers, and the multiplication facts.

I have about 300 baseball cards. You have about 400 baseball cards.

That means we have about 700 baseball cards.

Estimating to solve a problem

- **What's It Worth?** Give your child a number to write down. Then, ask for the value of each digit in the number. For example, ask your child to write "three hundred twenty-four." Then ask, "What is the value of the 3?" Your child should say, "three hundred."

- **Watch the Weather.** Encourage your child to listen to the weather report on the news. He or she may notice temperatures that are below zero in certain parts of the country. Encourage your child to look in the newspaper for daily temperatures reported around the world.

- **Multiplication Facts.** Help your child study the multiplication facts for the fives and tens using the *Triangle Flash Cards.*

Please contact me if you have any questions or comments.

Sincerely,

_____

UNIT OUTLINE

Numbers and Number Operations

Pacing Suggestions

Students' fluency with multiplication facts, their knowledge of place value, and their skills with addition and subtraction of whole numbers will determine how quickly the class can proceed through this unit. The following recommendations will help you adapt the unit to your students' needs.

- In Lesson 1 *Multiplying and Dividing with 5s and 10s* students assess their fluency with the multiplication facts and begin a systematic review of those facts that they need to study. They also begin work on the division facts. In this unit they review the multiplication facts and develop strategies for the division facts for the fives and tens. Work with the remaining groups of facts is distributed throughout the Daily Practice and Problems (DPP) and Home Practice in subsequent units. All students should continue learning new concepts and skills while they are working on the facts.

  Because the math facts program is closely linked to the recommended schedule for teaching lessons, classrooms that differ significantly from the suggested pacing will need to make accommodations in order to ensure that students receive a consistent program of math facts practice and assessment throughout the year. The *Grade 4 Facts Resource Guide* outlines a schedule for the study of the math facts in classrooms that move much more slowly through lessons than is recommended in the Lesson Guides. For more information, see the TIMS Tutor: *Math Facts* in the *Teacher Implementation Guide*.

The unit includes three optional lessons:

- **Lesson 2 *Roman Numerals*.** Use this lesson if your state or local standards suggest work with Roman numerals or other number systems. This lesson can also serve as an extension for students who show an interest in ancient number systems.

- **Lesson 3 *Place Value*.** This lesson includes an assessment that can be used to determine students' understanding of place value concepts. The lesson reviews place value and the use of base-ten pieces to represent numbers. All the concepts and skills in the lesson are included in the third grade materials. Use this lesson if your students have not had experiences using base-ten pieces to study place value or if the results of the assessment show that they need a review.

- **Lesson 6 *What's Below Zero?*** Use this lesson if your standards recommend that students study negative numbers. The lesson can also be used as an extension for students who do not need extensive work with math facts, place value, addition, or subtraction.

Components Key: SG = Student Guide, DAB = Discovery Assignment Book, AB = Adventure Book, URG = Unit Resource Guide, and DPP = Daily Practice and Problems

	Sessions	Description	Supplies
LESSON 1 **Multiplying and Dividing with 5s and 10s** SG pages 58–63 DAB pages 29–33 URG pages 20–29 DPP A–D	2	**ACTIVITY:** Students review the multiplication facts for fives and tens. This activity, along with the DPP for this unit, launches the yearlong math facts program that reviews the multiplication facts and develops fluency with the division facts.	• envelopes

	Sessions	Description	Supplies
LESSON 2		– OPTIONAL LESSON –	
Roman Numerals SG pages 64–67 URG pages 30–36	1	**OPTIONAL ACTIVITY:** Students learn about this ancient number system and compare it to their own.	
LESSON 3		– OPTIONAL LESSON –	
Place Value URG pages 37–45	1	**OPTIONAL ACTIVITY:** Students use connecting cubes to review place value concepts. **ASSESSMENT PAGE:** *Working with Base-Ten Pieces,* Unit Resource Guide, page 44.	• connecting cubes • base-ten pieces
LESSON 4			
The TIMS Candy Company SG pages 68–77 URG pages 46–60 DPP E–F	1–2	**ACTIVITY:** Students work with base-ten pieces to review and expand their understanding of place value.	• base-ten pieces
LESSON 5			
Addition and Subtraction SG pages 78–85 URG pages 61–75 DPP G–L	3	**ACTIVITY:** Students review and expand their understanding of addition and subtraction algorithms. **ASSESSMENT PAGE:** *Place Value Addition and Subtraction Quiz,* Unit Resource Guide, page 72.	• base-ten pieces
LESSON 6		– OPTIONAL LESSON –	
What's Below Zero? SG pages 86–91 DAB page 35 URG pages 76–84	1	**OPTIONAL ACTIVITY:** Students explore negative numbers in contexts such as temperature, altitudes, and bank balances. **ASSESSMENT PAGE:** *Professor Peabody Made a Mess!,* Unit Resource Guide, page 83.	• calculators • scissors • tape or glue

	Sessions	Description	Supplies
LESSON 7 **At the Hardware Store** SG pages 92–93 URG pages 85–92 DPP M–N	**1–2**	**ACTIVITY:** Students solve word problems based on concepts in this and previous units.	

CONNECTIONS

A current list of connections is available at www.mathtrailblazers.com.

Literature   **Suggested Titles**

- Burns, Marilyn. *The I Hate Mathematics! Book* Little, Brown, and Company, Boston, MA, 1976.
- Haskins, Jim. *Count Your Way through the Arab World,* illustrated by Dana Gustafson. Scott Foresman, Glenview, IL, 1988.
- Ifrah, Georges. *The Universal History of Numbers: From Prehistory to the Invention of the Computer.* John Wiley & Sons, Hoboken, NJ, 2000.
- Schmandt-Besserat, Denise. *The History of Counting.* Morrow Junior, New York, 1999.
- St. John, Glory. *How to Count Like a Martian.* Hill & Wang Publishing, New York, 1975.

Software

- *Ice Cream Truck* develops problem solving, money skills, and arithmetic operations.
- *Math Arena* is a collection of math activities that reinforces many math concepts.
- *Math Workshop Deluxe* develops math facts proficiency.
- *Mighty Math Calculating Crew* poses short answer questions about number operations and money skills.
- *National Library of Virtual Manipulatives* website (http://matti.usu.edu) allows students to work with manipulatives including base-ten pieces.
- *Schoolhouse Rock: Math Rock* develops number sense and math facts skills.

PREPARING FOR UPCOMING LESSONS

Place connecting cubes and base-ten pieces in a learning center for students to explore prior to beginning Lesson 3.

BACKGROUND

Numbers and Number Operations

This unit continues students' study of math facts and place value. It also reviews concepts and procedures for adding and subtracting whole numbers, including estimating sums and differences. Optional lessons provide introductions to Roman numerals and negative numbers.

Place Value

Students explore two key features of the base-ten number system. First, students gain a deeper understanding of the importance of position in our number system. In the number 326 we know that the 2 is 2 tens because only one digit is allowed in each position and each position has its own value. Second, students expand their understanding of trading ten units for one next-larger unit. We use base-ten pieces and base-ten shorthand, a written notation used to illustrate quantities of base-ten pieces, to help students visualize these concepts.

Initially, it takes longer to teach children place value and the algorithms by using the base-ten pieces than without them. The time is well-spent, however, and will save hours in the long run. Many older children do not understand place value. As a result, they make frequent computational errors by using a memorized algorithm incorrectly or inappropriately. They frequently need to be taught the algorithms over and over again.

Research has shown that if students over-practice procedures before they understand them, they have more difficulty making sense of them later. Programs that emphasize concept development can facilitate significant learning without sacrificing skill proficiency. (Hiebert, 1999) "Understanding makes learning skills easier, less susceptible to common errors, and less prone to forgetting." (National Research Council, p. 122, 2001) By building a solid conceptual foundation early and periodically reviewing place value concepts throughout the elementary school curriculum, student understanding and achievement will be greatly enhanced. (Suydam, 1986)

To start students thinking about the number system we use every day, they can first investigate the

Roman numeral system. The Roman system provides an example of a simpler grouping system without zero and is still used occasionally in our culture. Children enjoy reading Roman numerals on cornerstones of buildings, at the end of a movie's credits, and, of course, in reference to football Super Bowls. Also, experience comparing the Roman system to our modern version of the Hindu-Arabic system can provide students with a deeper understanding of the structure of our own base-ten system.

Students explore our number system by first reviewing the idea of grouping by tens using connecting cubes and working with small numbers. The connecting cubes allow students to actually snap ten individual cubes together to form a ten. Teachers report that students have difficulty understanding the trading that is done with base-ten pieces if they do not work with connecting cubes first. (Richardson, 1984) This intermediate activity helps students realize that ten ones is one ten. Base-ten pieces are then used to extend understanding of the addition and subtraction algorithms. If you feel your students have a good fundamental understanding of grouping and place value, then you may be able to omit Lessons 3 or 4. For more information, refer to Before the Activity in Lesson Guide 3 and the Pacing Suggestions in the Unit Outline.

Base-Ten Pieces

As in third grade, we use the imaginary TIMS Candy Company as a context for studying place value concepts. **Base-ten pieces** are used to keep track of how much candy is made. The individual pieces of candy are represented by **bits.** (See Figure 1.) When working with connecting cubes, these are the individual cubes. When working with base-ten pieces, they are the 1 cm × 1 cm × 1 cm cubes. When 10 bits are packaged together, they form a **skinny.** This is physically represented by 10 connecting cubes snapped together or by a tens piece (10 cm × 1 cm × 1 cm) in the base-ten pieces. When 10 skinnies are grouped together, they form a **flat** (a hundreds piece) and 10 flats make a **pack** (a thousands piece). The base-ten pieces have flats

(10 cm × 10 cm × 1 cm blocks) and packs (10 cm × 10 cm × 10 cm blocks). Connecting cubes are only used as individual bits and to form skinnies, not flats or packs.

We use nicknames (bits, skinnies, flats, and packs) for the base-ten pieces so that the concrete materials can be referred to separately from the numbers they represent. Also, in work with decimals in Unit 10, the value of the pieces is different. For example, the flat may be one whole, the skinny one-tenth, and the bit one-hundredth.

Base-Ten Shorthand

Children record their work with the base-ten pieces using base-ten shorthand and record their work numerically on the *Recording Sheets*. **Base-ten shorthand** is a pictorial representation of the base-ten pieces and is shown in Figure 1. In this way, concrete, pictorial, and symbolic representations are developed while still within the confines of a context. Concrete work with base-ten pieces helps students internalize the concept of place value. Research shows that helping students strengthen their abilities to move between different representations facilitates their acquisition of mathematical ideas and their problem-solving abilities. (Lesh, Post, and Behr, 1987)

Estimation

In this unit, students continue to develop their estimation skills. Ask students to think about the base-ten pieces when estimating. For example, to estimate $537 + 251$, think of the base-ten pieces that are used to model these two numbers. The most important unit, or piece, for 537 is the hundreds, i.e., 5 flats. For 251, the most important pieces are the 2 flats. The sum of the two numbers will be greater than 7 flats or 700. Estimating by looking at the largest unit is often referred to as **front-end estimation.** Students are also encouraged to find convenient numbers as discussed in Unit 1 Lesson 6.

Estimation skills develop gradually, and children need to develop for themselves a sense of when to estimate and how to estimate, lest they resort to memorization of procedures (Sowder, 1992). Many opportunities are provided for children to develop these skills. For more information on estimation, refer to the TIMS Tutor: *Estimation, Accuracy, and Error* in the *Teacher Implementation Guide.*

Math Facts

The Daily Practice and Problems (DPP) in Units 1 and 2 included assessments of students' proficiency with the addition and subtraction facts. Activities, games, and flash cards are provided for students

Nickname	Standard Name	Value	Picture	Shorthand
bit	one	1		.
skinny	ten	10		/
flat	hundred	100		
pack	thousand	1000		

Figure 1: *Base-ten pieces*

who need extra practice with these two groups of facts. See the Addition and Subtraction Math Facts Review in the *Grade 4 Facts Resource Guide* and the Daily Practice and Problems guides for Units 1 and 2.

The DPP for Unit 3 begins a review of the multiplication facts as well as a systematic, strategies-based approach for studying the division facts. For more information on the distribution of math facts practice, assessment, and descriptions of strategies, see the TIMS Tutor: *Math Facts* in the *Teacher*

Implementation Guide, the Daily Practice and Problems Guide in this unit, and the *Grade 4 Facts Resource Guide*.

Use the *Information for Parents: Grade 4 Math Facts Philosophy* to inform parents about the math facts program in Grade 4. This information sheet immediately follows the Background. A Spanish translation is included in the Letter Home Spanish Translation section of the *Unit Resource Guide File*.

Resources

- Bennett, A.B., Jr., and L.T. Nelson. *Mathematics for Elementary Teachers: A Conceptual Approach.* McGraw-Hill, Boston, 2001.
- Hiebert, J. "Relationships between Research and the NCTM Standards." *Journal for Research in Mathematics Education,* 30(1), pp. 3–19, 1999.
- Lesh, R., T. Post, and M. Behr. "Representations and Translations among Representations in Mathematics Learning and Problem Solving." In *Problems of Representation in the Teaching and Learning of Mathematics,* Claude Janvier (ed.). Lawrence Erlbaum Associates, Hillsdale, NJ, 1987.
- National Research Council. *Adding It Up: Helping Children Learn Mathematics.* J. Kilpatrick, J. Swafford, and B. Findell (eds.). National Academy Press, Washington, DC, 2001.
- *Principles and Standards for School Mathematics.* National Council of Teachers of Mathematics, Reston, VA, 2000.
- Richardson, K. *Developing Number Concepts Using Unifix Cubes.* Addison-Wesley, Menlo Park, CA, 1984.
- Sowder, J. "Estimation and Number Sense." In *Handbook of Research on Mathematics Teaching and Learning,* Douglas A. Grouws (ed.). Macmillan Publishing Company, New York, 1992.
- Suydam, M. "Manipulative Materials and Achievement." *Arithmetic Teacher,* 33 (6), pp. 10 and 32, 1986.

Assessment Indicators

- Can students name the value of a digit based on its place in a number?
- Can students represent two-, three-, and four-digit numbers using base-ten pieces?
- Can students represent addition and subtraction using base-ten pieces?
- Can students add multidigit numbers using paper and pencil?
- Can students subtract multidigit numbers using paper and pencil?
- Can students determine the reasonableness of a solution?
- Do students demonstrate fluency with the multiplication facts for the 5s and 10s?
- Can students write the four number sentences in the fact families for the 5s and 10s?

INFORMATION FOR PARENTS
Grade 4 Math Facts Philosophy

The goal of the math facts strand in *Math Trailblazers* is for students to learn the basic facts efficiently, gain fluency with their use, and retain that fluency over time. A large body of research supports an approach that is built on a foundation of work with strategies and concepts. This not only leads to more effective learning and better retention, but also leads to development of mental math skills. Therefore, the teaching of the basic facts in *Math Trailblazers* is characterized by the following elements:

Use of Strategies. Students first approach the basic facts as problems to be solved rather than as facts to be memorized. We encourage the use of strategies to find facts, so students become confident that they can find answers to fact problems that they do not immediately recall. In this way, students learn that math is more than memorizing facts and rules which "you either get or you don't."

Distributed Facts Practice. Students study small groups of facts that can be found using similar strategies. In fourth grade, the multiplication and division facts are divided into five groups. During the first semester students review the multiplication facts and develop strategies for the division facts, one group at a time. During the second semester, they review and practice the division facts in each group so that they can develop fluency with all of the facts by the end of the year. Practice of the five groups of facts is distributed throughout the curriculum and students are also given flash cards to practice groups of facts at home.

Practice in Context. Students learn the facts as they use them to solve problems in the labs, activities, and games.

Appropriate Assessment. Students are regularly assessed to determine whether they can find answers to fact problems quickly and accurately and whether they can retain this skill over time. A short quiz follows the study and review of each group of facts. Each student records his or her progress on *Facts I Know* charts and determines which facts he or she needs to study.

A Multiyear Approach. In Grades 1 and 2, the curriculum emphasizes the use of strategies that enable students to develop fluency with the addition and subtraction facts by the end of second grade. In Grade 3, they review the subtraction facts and begin strategy work with multiplication facts in order to achieve fluency by the end of the year. In Grade 4, the addition and subtraction facts are checked, the multiplication facts are reviewed, and fluency with the division facts is achieved. In Grade 5 all facts continue to be reviewed so as to retain fluency.

Facts Will Not Act as Gatekeepers. Use of strategies, calculators, and printed multiplication tables allows students to continue to work on interesting problems and experiments while they are learning the facts. Students are not prevented from learning more complex mathematics because they cannot perform well on facts tests.

OBSERVATIONAL ASSESSMENT RECORD

A1 Can students name the value of a digit based on its place in a number?

A2 Can students represent two-, three-, and four-digit numbers using base-ten pieces?

A3 Can students represent addition and subtraction using base-ten pieces?

A4 Can students add multidigit numbers using paper and pencil?

A5 Can students subtract multidigit numbers using paper and pencil?

A6 Can students determine the reasonableness of a solution?

A7 Do students demonstrate fluency with the multiplication facts for the 5s and 10s?

A8 Can students write the four number sentences in the fact families for the 5s and 10s?

A9 _____

Name	A1	A2	A3	A4	A5	A6	A7	A8	A9	Comments
1.										
2.										
3.										
4.										
5.										
6.										
7.										
8.										
9.										
10.										
11.										
12.										
13.										

Name	A1	A2	A3	A4	A5	A6	A7	A8	A9	Comments
14.										
15.										
16.										
17.										
18.										
19.										
20.										
21.										
22.										
23.										
24.										
25.										
26.										
27.										
28.										
29.										
30.										
31.										
32.										

Daily Practice and Problems

Numbers and Number Operations

A DPP Menu for Unit 3

Eight icons designate the subject matter of the Daily Practice and Problems (DPP) items. Each DPP item falls into one or more of the categories listed below. A brief menu of the DPP items included in Unit 3 follows.

N Number Sense F–K	**✖** Computation D, G–J	**🕐** Time E, K	**⬡** Geometry A, N
⁵⁄ₓ₇ Math Facts B, C, E, F, H, K–M	**$** Money B, D	**⚖** Measurement N	**📈** Data

Two DPP items are included for each nonoptional class session listed in the Unit Outline. The first item is always a Bit and the second is either a Task or a Challenge. Refer to the Daily Practice and Problems and Home Practice Guide in the *Teacher Implementation Guide* for further information on the DPP. This guide includes information on how and when to use the DPP. A Scope and Sequence Chart for the DPP for the year can be found in the *Teacher Implementation Guide.*

Practice and Assessment of the Multiplication and Division Facts

By the end of fourth grade, students in *Math Trailblazers* are expected to demonstrate fluency with all the multiplication and division facts. DPP items in Units 1 and 2 assessed proficiency with the addition and subtraction facts. The DPP for this unit begins a yearlong, systematic, strategies-based approach to reviewing the multiplication facts and learning and assessing the division facts.

In Units 3–8, students review the multiplication facts, studying them in the same five groups as they did in third grade. They review each group of multiplication facts in the context of fact families and in so doing, they begin to learn the related division facts. In Units 9–16, students concentrate on the division facts.

In Units 3–7, students assess their own fluency with the multiplication facts using *Triangle Flash Cards*

and the self-assessment page, *Multiplication Facts I Know* chart. Brief descriptions of these components are provided below. The table in Figure 2 lists the five groups of multiplication facts and shows the distribution of the flash cards and assessment for Units 3–8. A similar table for division facts is provided in Unit 9 for Units 9–16.

Sorting *Triangle Flash Cards.* When each fact group is introduced in the DPP, students are asked to practice their facts with a partner using *Triangle Flash Cards.* Students sort the cards into three piles: those they know and can answer quickly, those they can figure out with a strategy, and those that they need to learn. After sorting the flash cards, students should discuss the strategies they used to find the products.

***Multiplication Facts I Know* chart.** In this unit each student will begin a record of his or her progress with the multiplication facts. After sorting the flash cards, students record their current progress with the multiplication facts on their *Multiplication Facts I Know* charts by circling the facts they know and can answer quickly. Students are encouraged to update the chart when they practice the facts with the flash cards and after each quiz. They can also refer to the chart as a reference for facts they do not know as they encounter them. This chart is found in the *Discovery Assignment Book* and in the Generic Section. Students will begin a *Division Facts I Know* chart in Unit 8.

Quizzes and Inventory Tests. To assess students on each of the five groups of facts, short quizzes regularly appear as TIMS Bits in the DPP.

The short quizzes are less threatening to students and as effective as longer tests, so we strongly recommend against the use of weekly testing of 60 to 100 facts. In this unit, a quiz for the first group of multiplication facts (the 5s and 10s) is provided in item M. Unit 8 includes an inventory test on all five groups of facts. A second cycle of quizzes for division appears in the DPP for Units 9–15. Review of all of the facts will take place in Units 14 and 15.

Finally, Unit 16 includes a second inventory test with all the division facts.

For more information about the distribution and assessment of the math facts, see the TIMS Tutor: *Math Facts* in the *Teacher Implementation Guide* and the *Grade 4 Facts Resource Guide*. To inform parents about the curriculum's goals and philosophy of learning and assessing the math facts, send home a copy of the *Information for Parents: Grade 4 Math Facts Philosophy*, which immediately follows the Background for this unit.

Unit	Triangle Flash Cards: Group Organized by Strategy	Assessment
3	5s and 10s	• Sort flash cards and update *Multiplication Facts I Know* chart • Quiz and update chart
4	2s and 3s	• Sort flash cards and update *Multiplication Facts I Know* chart • Quiz and update chart
5	square numbers	• Sort flash cards and update *Multiplication Facts I Know* chart • Quiz and update chart
6	9s	• Sort flash cards and update *Multiplication Facts I Know* chart • Quiz and update chart
7	last six facts	• Sort flash cards and update *Multiplication Facts I Know* chart • Quiz and update chart
8	all five groups	• Inventory test on all five groups • Begin a *Division Facts I Know* chart for Units 9–16

Figure 2: *Distribution of flash cards and assessment of facts*

Daily Practice and Problems

UNIT 3

Students may solve the items individually, in groups, or as a class. The items may also be assigned for homework.

Student Questions	Teacher Notes

A Angles

Estimate. Name each angle as acute, obtuse, or right.

1.

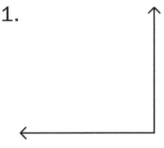

2.

3.

4.

TIMS Bit 🖾

Sketch the angles on the board.

1. right   2. obtuse

3. acute   4. obtuse

Discuss the answers by placing a corner of a book or piece of paper at the vertex of each angle.

B Nickels

What is the value of:

1. 5 nickels?

2. 8 nickels?

3. 6 dimes?

4. 2 dimes and 6 nickels?

How many nickels in:

5. 15¢

6. 45¢

7. 20¢

8. 35¢

TIMS Task $ 📇

1. 25¢   2. 40¢

3. 60¢   4. 50¢

5. 3   6. 9

7. 4   8. 7

URG · Grade 4 · Unit 3 · Daily Practice and Problems   13

Fact Families for × and ÷

Solve each pair of related facts. Then, name two other facts in the same fact family.

1. 5 × 2 =   10 ÷ 2 =

2. 5 × 6 =   30 ÷ 6 =

3. 5 × 5 =   25 ÷ 5 =

4. 10 × 7 =   70 ÷ 7 =

5. 10 × 4 =   40 ÷ 10 =

6. 10 × 10 =   100 ÷ 10 =

TIMS Bit

1. 10, 5, 2 × 5 = 10,
   10 ÷ 5 = 2

2. 30, 5, 6 × 5 = 30,
   30 ÷ 5 = 6

3. 25, 5, No other facts in this fact family; why?

4. 70, 10, 7 × 10 = 70,
   70 ÷ 10 = 7

5. 40, 4, 4 × 10 = 40,
   40 ÷ 4 = 10

6. 100, 10, No other facts in this fact family.

D **What Are Words Worth?**

Make yourself a chart where the letter A = 1¢, B = 2¢, C = 3¢, and so on until you get to Z = 26¢. You can now find the value of words by adding together the amounts for each letter in the word. For example, the word *cat* is worth 24¢ because C = 3¢, A = 1¢, and T = 20¢.

1. What is the value of the word *money*?

2. Which word is more valuable, *diamond* or *emerald*?

3. Try to find a word that is worth exactly $1.00.

4. Find the shortest word you can that is worth more than $1.00.

5. What is the most valuable word you can find?

TIMS Challenge

Encourage students to work together on this project. Questions 4 and 5 can be used as an ongoing class competition with the latest words posted in the room. Use of the dictionary and calculator is appropriate.

1. 72¢

2. diamond 60¢; emerald 58¢; diamond is more valuable.

3.–5. Answers will vary.

Time

1. Skip count by 5 minutes from 10:00 to 11:00.

2. Skip count by 10 minutes from 1:00 to 2:00.

3. How many minutes have gone by from 3:05 to 3:20?

4. How many minutes have gone by from 7:40 to 8:05?

TIMS Bit

1. 10:00, 10:05, 10:10, 10:15, 10:20, etc.

2. 1:00, 1:10, 1:20, 1:30, 1:40, 1:50, 2:00

3. 15 minutes

4. 25 minutes

 Story Solving

A. Write a story to show 5×7. Draw a picture to go with your story. Write a number sentence on your picture.

B. Write a story and a number sentence to show $35 \div 7$.

C. What are the other two facts in this fact family?

TIMS Task

A.–B. Answers will vary. For a sample story, students may refer to Question 3 on the *Multiplying and Dividing with 5s and 10s* Activity Pages in the *Student Guide*.

C. $7 \times 5 = 35$

   $35 \div 5 = 7$

Play *Digits Game* Addition

Draw boxes like these on your paper. As your teacher or classmate chooses the digits, place them in the boxes. Try to find the largest sum. Remember that each digit will be read only once.

☐ ☐ ☐

+ ☐ ☐

TIMS Bit

To begin the game, students draw the first set of boxes on their papers. The teacher chooses a digit at random from a set of *Digit Cards* (0–9). (*Digit Cards* can be found in the Generic Section of the *Unit Resource Guide*. As an alternative, you can use a deck of playing cards. The ace can stand for 1 and the joker or a face card can stand for zero.) Students place the digit in a box in such a way as to try to get the largest sum. Once a digit is placed, it can't be moved. Then, the teacher chooses a second digit without replacing the first. Play continues until the teacher has read enough digits. The player with the largest sum wins.

H **Fingers and Toes**

1. How many fingers are in the room right now? How many toes?

2. About how many fingers are in the school right now? About how many toes?

3. Explain how you solved Question 2.

4. There are 40 fingers around our table. How many hands are there? How many people?

TIMS Task

Answers will vary for Questions 1–3.

4. 8 hands
   4 people

Student Questions	Teacher Notes

 Play *Digits Game* Subtraction

Draw boxes like these on your paper. As your teacher or classmate chooses the digits, place them in the boxes. Try to find the largest difference. Remember that each digit will be read only once.

□ □ □
− □ □
‾‾‾‾‾‾‾

TIMS Bit

Students draw the second set of boxes on their paper. Play is similar to that described in item G; however, students try to find the largest difference.

 Take It Away!

Do these problems in your head.

1. 4003
   − 3997

2. 4007
   − 3995

3. 4001
   − 3800

4. 4000
   − 500

5. 4000
   − 501

6. 4000
   − 499

7. Explain your strategies for Question 1 and Question 5.

TIMS Task

These examples should encourage students to use counting up or other mental strategies rather than regrouping on paper. For example, in Question 1, a student might count up 3 from 3997 to 4000. Then, count up 3 more to 4003. Therefore, the answer is 6. In Question 5, a student might recall the answer for Question 4 (a similar problem) and take away one more number.

1. 6   2. 12

3. 201   4. 3500

5. 3499   6. 3501

7. Strategies will vary. See note above.

Skip Counting

1. Start on 0 and skip count by 5s on the calculator for 15 seconds.

2. Start on 0 and skip count by 10s on the calculator for 15 seconds. How far did you get?

TIMS Bit

1–2. Students should work in pairs for this activity.
To skip count by fives on the calculator, students should press:
5 + 5 = = = = = =, etc.
Calculators with the constant feature will repeat the operation, in this case adding five, each time the equal sign is pressed. Could they count twice as far by 10s as by 5s?

 Working with Fact Families for × and ÷

Solve the problems below and complete the number sentences for the related facts.

A. $5 \times 10 =$ _____

_____ $\div 5 =$ _____

_____ $\div 10 =$ _____

_____ $\times 5 =$ _____

B. $7 \times 5 =$ _____

_____ $\div 7 =$ _____

_____ $\div 5 =$ _____

_____ $\times 7 =$ _____

C. $3 \times 10 =$ _____

_____ $\div 3 =$ _____

_____ $\div 10 =$ _____

_____ $\times 10 =$ _____

D. $80 \div 8 =$ _____

_____ $\times 8 =$ _____

$80 \div$ _____ $=$ _____

$8 \times$ _____ $=$ _____

E. $20 \div 5 =$ _____

_____ $\times 5 =$ _____

$5 \times$ _____ $=$ _____

$20 \div$ _____ $=$ _____

F. $10 \times 9 =$ _____

_____ $\div 9 =$ _____

_____ $\div$ _____ $= 9$

$9 \times$ _____ $=$ _____

TIMS Task

A. $5 \times 10 = 50, 50 \div 5 = 10,$
   $50 \div 10 = 5, 10 \times 5 = 50$

B. $7 \times 5 = 35, 35 \div 7 = 5,$
   $35 \div 5 = 7, 5 \times 7 = 35$

C. $3 \times 10 = 30, 30 \div 3 = 10,$
   $30 \div 10 = 3, 3 \times 10 = 30$

D. $80 \div 8 = 10, 10 \times 8 = 80,$
   $80 \div 10 = 8, 8 \times 10 = 80$

E. $20 \div 5 = 4, 4 \times 5 = 20,$
   $5 \times 4 = 20, 20 \div 4 = 5$

F. $10 \times 9 = 90, 90 \div 9 = 10,$
   $90 \div 10 = 9, 9 \times 10 = 90$

Student Questions	Teacher Notes

 Quiz on 5s and 10s

A. 5 × 2 =   B. 3 × 10 =   C. 5 × 5 =

D. 8 × 10 =   E. 6 × 10 =   F. 5 × 3 =

G. 10 × 9 =   H. 7 × 5 =   I. 10 × 2 =

J. 10 × 7 =   K. 6 × 5 =   L. 5 × 10 =

M. 8 × 5 =   N. 9 × 5 =   O. 4 × 10 =

P. 4 × 5 =   Q. 10 × 10 =

TIMS Bit

This quiz is on the first group of multiplication facts, the 5s and 10s. We recommend 2 minutes for this test. You might want to allow students to change pens after the time is up and complete the remaining problems in a different color.

After students take the test, have them update their *Multiplication Facts I Know* charts.

 Antopolis Airport

Below is a sketch of the hangar at Antopolis Airport. (Planes are stored and repaired in hangars.)

Find the area and perimeter of the hangar. You may wish to build the hangar with square-inch tiles.

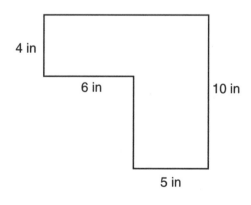

TIMS Challenge

The floor's area is 74 sq inches. The perimeter is 42 inches. One way to solve this problem is to divide the floor into two rectangles as shown. Students may actually build the floor of the hangar with the square-inch tiles.

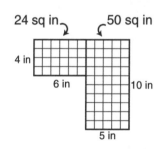

LESSON GUIDE 1

Multiplying and Dividing with 5s and 10s

Estimated Class Sessions: 2

This lesson introduces the yearlong review of the multiplication facts and launches the systematic strategies-based approach to learning the division facts. Students solve word problems to develop and enhance their understanding of the division operation. Fact families are introduced so students can use multiplication facts to learn related division facts. They use flash cards to assess their fluency with multiplication facts for the fives and tens. They study multiplication with zero and one.

Key Content

- Self-assessing the multiplication and division facts for the 5s and 10s.
- Using known multiplication facts to learn related division facts.
- Multiplying by 0 and 1.
- Writing the four related number sentences in a fact family.

Key Vocabulary

dividend
division sentence
divisor
fact family
factors
product
quotient
turn-around facts

Curriculum Sequence

Before This Unit

In third grade, students studied all the multiplication facts. They explored division concepts in Grade 3 Units 7, 11, and 19. Students explored multiplication by zero and one in the Adventure Book story *Cipher Force* in Grade 3 Unit 11 Lesson 7.

After This Unit

Students continue reviewing the multiplication facts and develop strategies for the division facts in Units 4–8. In Units 9–16, they develop fluency with the division facts while maintaining their fluency with the multiplication facts.

Materials List

Print Materials for Students

	Math Facts and Daily Practice and Problems	Activity	Homework
Student Guide *(Student Books)*		*Multiplying and Dividing with 5s and 10s* Pages 58–62	*Multiplying and Dividing with 5s and 10s* Homework Section Page 63
Discovery Assignment Book *(Student Books)*		*Triangle Flash Cards: 5s* Page 29, *Triangle Flash Cards: 10s* Page 31, and *Multiplication Facts I Know,* Page 33	Home Practice Parts 1 & 4 Pages 23 & 25
Facts Resource Guide *(Teacher Resources)* ◎	DPP Items 3B & 3C Use *Triangle Flash Cards: 5s* and *Triangle Flash Cards: 10s* to review the multiplication facts for the 5s and 10s		
Unit Resource Guide *(Teacher Resources)*	DPP Items A–D Pages 13–14 *Information for Parents: Grade 4 Math Facts Philosophy* Page 8 ◎		
Generic Section *(Teacher Resources)* ◎			*Triangle Flash Cards: 5s* and *Triangle Flash Cards: 10s,* 1 each per student (optional)

◎ *available on Teacher Resource CD*

All Transparency Masters, Blackline Masters, and Assessment Blackline Masters in the Unit Resource Guide are on the Teacher Resource CD.

Supplies for Each Student

1 or 2 envelopes for storing flash cards

Materials for the Teacher

Transparencies of *Triangle Flash Cards: 5s* and *Triangle Flash Cards: 10s* (Discovery Assignment Book) Pages 29 and 31

TIMS Tip

For more durable flash cards, copy the *Triangle Flash Cards* in the Generic Section onto card stock or laminate the cards. You may also give students two sets of cards so that they can take a set home and leave a set at school.

Content Note

In Units 3–7, students use the *Triangle Flash Cards* and the *Facts I Know* charts only with the multiplication facts. They will build strategies for the division facts in Units 3–8 and use the *Triangle Flash Cards* to develop fluency with the division facts in Units 8–16. Reviewing the multiplication facts will facilitate their work with the division facts. Students will use the same groups of flash cards to study the division facts in Units 9–16.

Multiplying and Dividing with 5s and 10s

Using Fact Families – Multiplying and Dividing with 5s and 10s

Jackson's Hardware Store decided to donate 30 basketballs to the schools in the neighborhood.

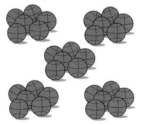

John and his father went to pick up the basketballs for Bessie Coleman school. When they arrived at the store there were people from four other schools waiting to pick up their basketballs. John helped divide the thirty basketballs into five groups.

Each of the 5 schools got 6 new basketballs.

The **division sentence** for this is 30 ÷ 5 = 6. The answer to a division problem is called the **quotient**. In this sentence the quotient is six. Thirty, or the number to be divided, is the **dividend**. The **divisor** is five.

58   SG · Grade 4 · Unit 3 · Lesson 1   *Multiplying and Dividing with 5s and 10s*

Student Guide - Page 58

Before the Activity

Part 3 of this lesson introduces students to *Triangle Flash Cards.* The *Triangle Flash Cards* for the 5s and 10s are located in the *Discovery Assignment Book.* Have students cut out the cards from their books and place them in envelopes.

Developing the Activity

Part 1. Using Fact Families: Multiplying and Dividing with 5s and 10s

The vignette on the first page of the *Multiplying and Dividing with 5s and 10s* Activity Pages in the *Student Guide* presents a situation that illustrates the relationship between two facts ($30 \div 5 = 6$ and $5 \times 6 = 30$). It introduces students to the use of **fact families.** Students should see that division is the opposite (inverse) operation of multiplication.

Multiplication can be thought of as repeated addition, for example, adding five groups of six for a total of 30 basketballs. Division can be thought of as repeated subtraction, for example, subtracting five groups of six basketballs from 30.

Discuss *Question 1* in the *Student Guide.* Ask:

*   *What information is given in the problem?* (The total number of soccer balls, 30, and the number of balls in each group, 6.)
*   *What does the answer, the* **quotient,** *tell you?* (The number of schools that will receive soccer balls.)
*   *How is* **Question 1** *different from the basketball story? Think about what the problem tells you and what you need to find out.* (In the story we know the number of schools, 5, and we want to find out the number of basketballs for each school, 6. In *Question 1* we know the number of soccer balls each school will receive, 6, and we want to know how many schools will receive them, 5.)
*   *What number sentence represents the basketball story?* ($30 \div 5 = 6$)
*   *What is a number sentence for the soccer ball problem?* ($30 \div 6 = 5$)
*   *How are they alike?* (They have the same numbers. Thirty is the **dividend** in both sentences.)
*   *How are they different?* (The **divisors** and quotients change. Thirty basketballs are divided into five groups in the basketball story. Thirty soccer balls are divided into groups of six in the soccer ball problem.)

- *How can we check a division problem? Give me an example.* (Multiply the quotient by the divisor. To check 30 ÷ 6 = 5, multiply 5 times 6 to get 30.)
- *What can we say about multiplication and division together?* (They are opposites. They "undo" each other.)

Write all four number sentences on the board or the overhead projector. Tell students that the four related sentences make a **fact family.**

$$5 \times 6 = 30 \qquad 6 \times 5 = 30$$
$$30 \div 5 = 6 \qquad 30 \div 6 = 5$$

Remind students that the two multiplication sentences are **turn-around facts** (5 × 6 and 6 × 5). Students should remember turn-around facts from third grade.

Ask students to work through *Questions 2–5* in pairs. *Questions 2–4* provide different division situations. Having students draw pictures reinforces their understanding of the concept represented by the number sentences. For *Question 5,* students should understand that knowing one member of a fact family helps them learn the other members of the same fact family.

Questions 6–15 provide practice with fact families. They require students to use math facts in the context of money and other contexts. These questions can also be assigned for homework.

Journal Prompt

Why do you think we call four facts like these
(5 × 6 = 30, 6 × 5 = 30, 30 ÷ 5 = 6, 30 ÷ 6 = 5)
a fact family?

Content Note

Division can be applied to two types of situations. The first is called partitive (sharing) division and is applied to problems like the basketball giveaway story. The total number of objects and the desired number of groups (partitions) are known. What is not known and what will be determined by the answer is the number of objects in each group. Thirty basketballs shared among five schools results in six basketballs per school.

The second type of division situation is known as measurement (subtractive) division. It is illustrated by *Question 1* in the *Student Guide.* In this case, the total number of objects to be distributed and the size (or measure) of the groups are known. What is not known and what will be determined by the answer is the number of groups that will result. Thirty soccer balls divided into groups of six balls each results in five groups.

The labels for these two situations are not important here. However, it is important for students to have opportunities to solve both types of problems.

Then John told everyone that he would label all the basketballs with the correct school name. Everyone brought the new basketballs back to him for labeling, one school at a time. John added 6 + 6 + 6 + 6 + 6. He knew this was the same as five groups of six or 5 times 6, or 30 basketballs in all.

John knew that 5 × 6 = 30 is related to the division sentence 30 ÷ 5 = 6. There are two more sentences that are related: 6 × 5 = 30 and 30 ÷ 6 = 5. We call all four of these sentences together a **fact family.**

1. Jackson's Hardware also gave away a total of 30 soccer balls. Each school received a crate of six balls.
   A. How many schools got soccer balls? Write a number sentence to describe this.
   B. What does each number in the sentence represent?

2. John found he had 30 marbles at home and decided to give an equal number of marbles to each of his three sisters. How many marbles did John give to each sister? Draw a picture for this problem and describe it using a division sentence. Write another number sentence that is in the same fact family.

3. Nila wrote a division story for 20 ÷ 5. Nila drew a picture for her story.

   A. What is another number sentence that is in the same fact family as 20 ÷ 5?
   B. Write a division story for 50 ÷ 10. Draw a picture for your story and write a number sentence. Write three more sentences that are in the same fact family.

Student Guide - Page 59

---

4. Maya baked chocolate chip cookies. She counted out 45 cookies and put an equal number in each of 9 bags. Then she gave one bag of cookies to 9 friends.
   A. How many cookies did she give each friend? Write a number sentence for this story.
   B. Write a multiplication number sentence in the same fact family. What do the numbers in the multiplication sentence represent?

5. Which of the following number sentences is in the same fact family as 5 × 8 = 40?
   a) 40 ÷ 10 = 4   b) 40 ÷ 5 = 8   c) 8 × 4 = 32   d) 8 × 5 = 40

Solve Questions 6–15. Use fact families, manipulatives, or other strategies. Write a number sentence for each problem. Then write the other three sentences in the fact family.

6. How many dimes are in 80 cents?

7. How many nickels are in 35 cents?

8. How many nickels are in 15 cents?

9. How many nickels are in 40 cents?

10. How many dimes are in 60 cents?

11. How many nickels are in 20 cents?

12. How many dimes are in 40 cents?

13. Maya gets paid for helping her neighbor with her baby one afternoon each week. She saves all the money she gets and after five weeks, she has $25. How much money does Maya get paid each week? Write a number sentence.

14. How many weeks will Maya have to help her neighbor to make $45? Write a number sentence.

15. John lives 4 blocks from school. It takes him 20 minutes to walk to school. If John walks steadily, how long does it take John to walk one block? Write a number sentence.

Student Guide - Page 60

Multiplying with 0 and 1

16. Think about multiplication as repeated addition of groups. Three groups of five makes fifteen. $3 \times 5 = 15$. Now think about what happens when you multiply with 1 or 0. How many groups do you have? How many are in each group? Try the following problems. You may want to use your calculator.

A. $5 \times 0 =$ 　　　　B. $5 \times 1 =$

C. $10 \times 0 =$ 　　　D. $1 \times 10 =$

E. $0 \times 98 =$ 　　　F. $98 \times 1 =$

G. $0 \times 5348 =$ 　　H. $1 \times 5348 =$

17. A. What can you say about multiplying numbers by 0? Explain.
    B. What can you say about multiplying numbers by 1? Explain.

Multiplication Facts and *Triangle Flash Cards*

With a partner, use the directions below and your *Triangle Flash Cards: 5s* and *Triangle Flash Cards: 10s* to practice the multiplication facts.

- One partner covers the shaded number, the largest number on the card. This number will be the answer to the multiplication problem. It is called the **product.**
- The second person multiplies the two uncovered numbers (one in a circle, one in a square). These are the two **factors.** It does not matter which of the factors is said first.
4×5 and 5×4 both equal 20.
$4 \times 5 = 20$ and $5 \times 4 = 20$ are called **turn-around facts.**

$5 \times 4 = ?$

$4 \times 5 = ?$

Multiplying and Dividing with 5s and 10s 　　　　SG · Grade 4 · Unit 3 · Lesson 1 　61

- Separate the facts into three piles: those facts you know and can answer quickly, those that you can figure out with a strategy, and those that you need to learn.
- Discuss how you can figure out facts that you do not recall right away. Share your strategies with your partner.
- Practice the last two piles again and then make a list of the facts you need to practice at home for homework.
- Circle the facts you know quickly on your *Multiplication Facts I Know* chart. Remember that if you know one fact, you also know its turn-around fact. Circle both on your chart.
- Review your answers to Question 17.
- You will continue to use *Triangle Flash Cards* to study other groups of facts. If you know one or two of the multiplication facts in a fact family, you can use those facts to help you learn the division facts.

Multiplication Facts I Know

×	0	1	2	3	4	5	6	7	8	9	10
0	0	0	0	0	0	0	0	0	0	0	0
1	0	1	2	3	4	5	6	7	8	9	10
2	0	2	4	6	8	10	12	14	16	18	20
3	0	3	6	9	12	15	18	21	24	27	30
4	0	4	8	12	16	20	24	28	32	36	40
5	0	5	10	15	20	25	30	35	40	45	50
6	0	6	12	18	24	30	36	42	48	54	60
7	0	7	14	21	28	35	42	49	56	63	70
8	0	8	16	24	32	40	48	56	64	72	80
9	0	9	18	27	36	45	54	63	72	81	90
10	0	10	20	30	40	50	60	70	80	90	100

62　SG · Grade 4 · Unit 3 · Lesson 1 　　　　Multiplying and Dividing with 5s and 10s

Part 2. Multiplying with 0 and 1

Have students complete *Questions 16–17* in pairs before discussing them together as a class. Continue the discussion:

- *How can both 5×0 and 10×0 equal the same answer?* (Possible response: Five groups of zero objects and ten groups of zero objects are both zero.)

- *Make up a number story about* **Question 16D.** (One possible story: Jackson's Hardware Store gave away one box of ten Ping-Pong balls. How many balls did the store give away?)

- *What is one times ten million? How do you know?* (ten million. One group of ten million is just ten million.)

- *What is the product of one and any number? How do you know?* (that number. Because one group of any number is that number.)

- *What is zero times ten million? How do you know?* (zero. If I have zero groups of ten million, I have zero.)

- *What is the product of any number and zero? How do you know?* (zero. Repeated addition of zero any number of times is zero and zero groups of any number is still zero.)

Part 3. Multiplication Facts and Triangle Flash Cards

The *Student Guide* outlines how students use the *Triangle Flash Cards* for multiplication, and Part 1 of the Home Practice in the *Discovery Assignment Book* provides a quick review. Partners cover the number that is shaded (the largest number on the card). This is the **product,** the answer to the multiplication problem that the other two numbers (the **factors**) present. The student who is being quizzed multiplies the two numbers that are showing, gives the answer, and the answer is checked.

As their partners quiz them on the facts, students sort the cards into three piles—those facts they know and can answer quickly, those facts they know using a strategy, and those facts they need to learn. Then each student begins his or her *Multiplication Facts I Know* chart found in the *Discovery Assignment Book*. Students circle only those facts that they know and can answer quickly. However, remind students that if they know a fact, they also know its turn-around fact. So, if they circle $5 \times 3 = 15$, they can also circle $3 \times 5 = 15$. Also remind students of the discussion of multiplication by zero and one. Using what they learned from *Questions 16* and *17*, they can circle the facts for zero and one. Students make a list of the facts for the fives and tens that they did not circle on their charts. They take this list home along with their flash cards so that they can practice the facts they need to study with a family member.

Students will work with the *Triangle Flash Cards* for the division facts in Units 9–16 and record their progress on a *Division Facts I Know* chart at that time. Until then, they use flash cards and the chart primarily for multiplication facts. At the same time, students are practicing division facts in activities, labs, and the Daily Practice and Problems. As students review the multiplication facts through practice with fact families, they will see their fluency with the division facts increase.

DPP items B, C, E, F, H, K, and L provide further practice with the multiplication and division facts for the fives and tens. A quiz on the multiplication facts for the fives and tens is provided in Bit M. Inform students when the quiz will be given so they can practice at home. As students encounter multiplication problems with the facts, encourage them to share their strategies. The fives and tens are easily solved using skip counting. For descriptions of other multiplication facts strategies, see the TIMS Tutor: *Math Facts* in the *Teacher Implementation Guide*.

Content Note

This lesson illustrates the following mathematical properties:

Identity Property of Multiplication. This is also known as the Property of One for Multiplication. One times any number is that number. Using variables, $n \times 1 = n$.

Zero Property of Multiplication. Any number times zero is zero. Using variables, $n \times 0 = 0$.

Commutative Property of Multiplication. This is also known as the Order Property of Multiplication. Changing the order of the factors does not change the product. For example, $3 \times 5 = 5 \times 3 = 15$. Using variables, $n \times m = m \times n$.

It is not necessary at this point that students know the names of these properties or be able to state them using variables. It is sufficient that they can use the ideas when they solve problems.

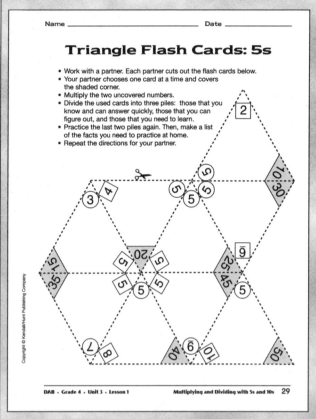

Discovery Assignment Book - Page 29

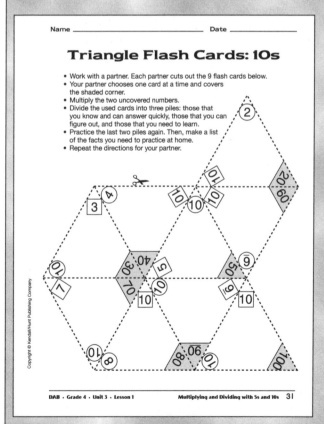

Discovery Assignment Book - Page 31

Daily Practice and Problems:
Task and Challenge for Lesson 1

B. Task: Nickels (URG p. 13)

What is the value of:

1. 5 nickels?
2. 8 nickels?
3. 6 dimes?
4. 2 dimes and 6 nickels?

How many nickels in:

5. 15¢
6. 45¢
7. 20¢
8. 35¢

D. Challenge: What Are Words Worth? (URG p. 14)

Make yourself a chart where the letter A = 1¢, B = 2¢, C = 3¢, and so on until you get to Z = 26¢. You can now find the value of words by adding together the amounts for each letter in the word. For example, the word *cat* is worth 24¢ because C = 3¢, A = 1¢, and T = 20¢.

1. What is the value of the word *money*?

2. Which word is more valuable, *diamond or emerald?*

3. Try to find a word that is worth exactly $1.00.

4. Find the shortest word you can that is worth more than $1.00.

5. What is the most valuable word you can find?

Content Note

Because the math facts program is closely linked to the recommended schedule for teaching lessons, classrooms that differ significantly from the suggested pacing will need to make accommodations in order to ensure that students receive a consistent program of math facts practice and assessment throughout the year. The *Grade 4 Facts Resource Guide* outlines a schedule for math facts practice and assessment in classrooms that are moving much more slowly through lessons than is recommended in the lesson guides. The *Grade 4 Facts Resource Guide* contains all components of the math facts program, including DPP items, flash cards, *Facts I Know* charts, and assessments.

Suggestions for Teaching the Lesson

Math Facts

- In Task B, students use math facts to solve problems involving nickels and dimes. Bit C provides practice with fact families.

- Part 1 of the Home Practice reminds students to take home their flash cards for the fives and tens. Students may practice these facts with a family member. Also send home the *Information for Parents: Grade 4 Math Facts Philosophy.* This information sheet can be found immediately following the Background.

- Part 4 of the Home Practice provides additional practice with fact families.

Answers for Part 4 of the Home Practice can be found in the Answer Key at the end of this lesson and at the end of this unit.

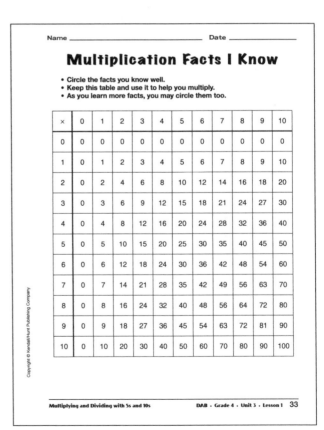

Discovery Assignment Book - Page 33

Homework and Practice

- Assign homework *Questions 1–10* in the *Student Guide*.
- DPP Bit A provides practice identifying acute, obtuse, and right triangles.

Extension

Item D challenges students to find the value of words if an A is worth 1¢, a B is worth 2¢, and so on. Students enjoy solving the problems while practicing addition and estimation.

Homework

Dear Family Member:

Your child is reviewing the multiplication facts and learning the division facts for fives and tens by studying fact families. For example, 5 × 4 = 20, 4 × 5 = 20, 20 ÷ 5 = 4, 20 ÷ 4 = 5 is a fact family. Once a student learns the multiplication facts, learning the division facts becomes easier. Using fact families is a good strategy for solving most of the problems below. Remind your child to bring home the flash cards for the fives and tens. Help him or her study these facts.

Thank you for your cooperation.

1. How many dimes in 90 cents?

2. How many nickels in 30 cents?

3. Banks wrap dimes into packs of 50 dimes. If Nila takes 70 dimes to the bank to be wrapped, how many packs will she get? How many dollars will this be? How many dimes will be left over?

4. There are 20 Little League teams in the city. The League places 10 teams in a division. How many divisions will there be in the city? Write a number sentence for this story and all the number sentences in this fact family.

5. Write a story to show 45 ÷ 9. Draw a picture to go with your story and write a number sentence. Write all the other number sentences that are in this fact family.

6. Show two ways you can have 25 cents if you have only dimes and nickels.

7. Show three ways you can have 40 cents if you have only dimes and nickels.

8. Chewy Candies come in packs of five. Irma has 3 packs, Michael has 5 packs, Romesh has 1 pack, and Jessie has no packs.

   A. How many candies does each student have? Write a number sentence for each student.

   B. How many candies do they have altogether?

9. Jacob has 60 cents and needs $1.00 for a show. How many dimes does he need to make $1.00?

10. A pack of Chewy Candies costs 15 cents. How many packs can you buy with $1.00? Explain your solution.

Multiplying and Dividing with 5s and 10s　　　　　SG · Grade 4 · Unit 3 · Lesson 1　63

Student Guide - Page 63

Name _____ Date _____

Unit 3: Home Practice

Part 1　Triangle Flash Cards: 5s and 10s
Study for the quiz on the multiplication facts for the fives and tens. Take home your *Triangle Flash Cards: 5s and 10s* and your list of facts you need to study.

Here's how to use the flash cards. Ask a family member to choose one flash card at a time. He or she should cover the corner containing the highest number. This number will be the answer to a multiplication problem. Multiply the two uncovered numbers.

Study the math facts in small groups. Choose to study 8 to 10 facts each night. Your teacher will tell you when the quiz on the fives and tens will be.

Part 2　Addition and Subtraction
Use paper and pencil to solve the following problems.

1. 644	2. 76	3. 386	4. 196
+ 53	+ 29	− 21	− 77

5. 938	6. 4015	7. 5048	8. 4653
− 449	+ 488	− 274	+ 5664

Choose one problem. Be ready to explain how you can tell if the answer is reasonable.

NUMBERS AND NUMBER OPERATIONS　　　　DAB · Grade 4 · Unit 3　23

Discovery Assignment Book - Page 23

Name _____ Date _____

Part 4　Fact Families
For each fact given, write the other three members of the same fact family.

A. 6 × 5 = 30　　_____
　　　　　　　　　_____
　　　　　　　　　_____

B. 90 ÷ 10 = 9　　_____
　　　　　　　　　_____
　　　　　　　　　_____

C. 15 ÷ 5 = 3　　_____
　　　　　　　　　_____
　　　　　　　　　_____

D. 5 × 9 = 45　　_____
　　　　　　　　　_____
　　　　　　　　　_____

E. 5 × 10 = 50　　_____
　　　　　　　　　_____
　　　　　　　　　_____

NUMBERS AND NUMBER OPERATIONS　　　　DAB · Grade 4 · Unit 3　25

Discovery Assignment Book - Page 25

AT A GLANCE

Math Facts and Daily Practice and Problems

DPP Bit A reviews angles. Items B and C provide practice with the multiplication and division facts for the fives and tens. Challenge D is a problem-solving activity.

Before the Activity

Students cut out the *Triangle Flash Cards: 5s* and *10s* from the *Discovery Assignment Book* and store them in envelopes.

Part 1. Using Fact Families: Multiplying and Dividing with 5s and 10s

1. Students are introduced to fact families and begin learning their division facts for the fives and tens.
2. Students discuss the relationship between multiplication and division *(Question 1)*.
3. Students work on *Questions 2–5* in pairs and then share their answers with the class.
4. Students practice with fact families *(Questions 6–15)*.

Part 2. Multiplying with 0 and 1

Students explore multiplication with 0 and 1 *(Questions 16–17)*.

Part 3. Multiplication Facts and *Triangle Flash Cards*

Students review the multiplication facts for the fives and tens by using *Triangle Flash Cards*.

Homework

1. Assign Parts 1 and 4 of the Home Practice.
2. Assign *Questions 1–10* in the Homework section of the *Student Guide*.

Assessment

Students begin a record of their progress with the facts by using the *Multiplication Facts I Know* chart in the *Discovery Assignment Book*.

Notes:

Student Guide

Questions 1–17 (SG pp. 59–61)

1.* **A.** 5 schools; $30 \div 6 = 5$

   B. 30 soccer balls, 6 balls in a crate, 5 schools

2.* 10 marbles; $30 \div 3 = 10$. Other sentences in the same fact family are $30 \div 10 = 3$, $3 \times 10 = 30$, $10 \times 3 = 30$.

3.* **A.** Possible answers: $20 \div 4 = 5$, $4 \times 5 = 20$, $5 \times 4 = 20$.

   B. Answers will vary.

4.* **A.** 5 cookies, $45 \div 9 = 5$

   B. $5 \times 9 = 45$ (or $9 \times 5 = 45$) 5 cookies in a bag, 9 bags (or 9 friends), 45 cookies in all

5. b and d are in the same fact family

6. 8 dimes, $80 \div 10 = 8$, $80 \div 8 = 10$, $10 \times 8 = 80$, $8 \times 10 = 80$

7. 7 nickels, $35 \div 5 = 7$, $35 \div 7 = 5$, $7 \times 5 = 35$, $5 \times 7 = 35$

8. 3 nickels, $15 \div 5 = 3$, $15 \div 3 = 5$, $3 \times 5 = 15$, $5 \times 3 = 15$

9. 8 nickels, $40 \div 5 = 8$, $40 \div 8 = 5$, $8 \times 5 = 40$, $5 \times 8 = 40$

10. 6 dimes, $60 \div 10 = 6$, $60 \div 6 = 10$, $6 \times 10 = 60$, $10 \times 6 = 60$

11. 4 nickels, $20 \div 5 = 4$, $20 \div 4 = 5$, $5 \times 4 = 20$, $4 \times 5 = 20$

12. 4 dimes, $40 \div 10 = 4$, $40 \div 4 = 10$, $4 \times 10 = 40$, $10 \times 4 = 40$

13. $25 \div 5 = 5$ dollars per week

14. $45 \div 5 = 9$ weeks

15. $20 \div 4 = 5$ minutes

16.* **A.** 0   **B.** 5

   C. 0   **D.** 10

   E. 0   **F.** 98

   G. 0   **H.** 5348

17.* **A.** Any number multiplied by 0 is 0. Zero groups of any number is zero.

   B. Any number multiplied by 1 is the number itself. One group of any number is that number.

Homework

Questions 1–10 (SG p. 63)

1. 9 dimes

2. 6 nickels

3. 1 pack of dimes, $5.00, and 20 dimes left over ($2.00).

4. 2 divisions in the city; $20 \div 10 = 2$. Other number sentences in the fact family are $20 \div 2 = 10$, $2 \times 10 = 20$, $10 \times 2 = 20$.

5. Answers will vary. The other number sentences in the same fact family are $45 \div 5 = 9$, $5 \times 9 = 45$, $9 \times 5 = 45$.

6. Two dimes and one nickel, one dime and three nickels.

7. Three dimes and two nickels, two dimes and four nickels, one dime and six nickels.

8. **A.** Irma had 15 candies, Michael had 25 candies, Romesh had 5 candies, and Jessie had no candy. $3 \times 5 = 15$, $5 \times 5 = 25$, $1 \times 5 = 5$, $0 \times 5 = 0$.

   B. 45 candies

9. 4 dimes

10. 6 packs. Possible strategy: 2 packs cost 30¢. $30¢ \times 3 = 90¢$. So 6 packs cost 90¢.

Discovery Assignment Book

**Home Practice (DAB p. 25)

Part 4. Fact Families

Questions A–E

A. $30 \div 5 = 6$, $5 \times 6 = 30$, $30 \div 6 = 5$

B. $9 \times 10 = 90$, $10 \times 9 = 90$, $90 \div 9 = 10$

C. $3 \times 5 = 15$, $15 \div 3 = 5$, $5 \times 3 = 15$

D. $9 \times 5 = 45$, $45 \div 5 = 9$, $45 \div 9 = 5$

E. $10 \times 5 = 50$, $50 \div 5 = 10$, $50 \div 10 = 5$

*Answers and/or discussion are included in the Lesson Guide.

**Answers for all the Home Practice in the *Discovery Assignment Book* are at the end of the unit.

OPTIONAL LESSON

LESSON GUIDE

Roman Numerals

Estimated Class Sessions: 1

Students work with the Roman numeral system in order to better understand our Hindu-Arabic system.

There are no Daily Practice and Problems items for this lesson.

Key Content

- Writing Roman numerals.
- Recognizing key elements of the Hindu-Arabic system.
- Recognizing and using patterns to write numbers.

Key Vocabulary

Roman numerals
subtractive principle

Materials List

Print Materials for Students

Student Book	Student Guide	Optional Activity	Homework
		Roman Numerals Pages 64–67	Roman Numerals Homework Section Page 67

available on Teacher Resource CD

All Transparency Masters, Blackline Masters, and Assessment Blackline Masters in the Unit Resource Guide are on the Teacher Resource CD.

Materials for the Teacher

Transparency of the Roman Numerals and Symbols chart from the *Roman Numerals* Activity Pages (Student Guide) Page 65, optional

Developing the Activity

This activity gives students historical perspective on the development of numbers. The number system we use developed over many years, drew from the advancements made by many peoples, and bears similarities to other numbering systems.

The Roman system is well-suited for discussion of how numerals have evolved. Like our system, it is based on ten. However, we use different symbols for each of the first ten numbers and form all the rest of our numbers using those ten digits. We rely on the position of the digit to clarify its value. The Roman system uses different symbols to show groups as part of the total such as putting V and III together (VIII) to denote eight. This organization is much closer to early grouping systems. Although the Romans generally organized their symbols by value (placing the ones, tens, hundreds, etc., together) and placing the symbols with the largest value at the left, the Roman system is not a true place value system.

Have students read about Roman numerals on the *Roman Numerals* Activity Pages in the *Student Guide.* Use the chart of Roman Numerals and Symbols on these pages to discuss further how Roman numerals evolved.

Explain to students that the symbols they are likely to see used today are those listed in the second column of the chart. Use the chart to discuss with students the possible sources of the Roman numerals we use today.

Use the modern symbols on the chart to translate some examples of Hindu-Arabic numbers into Roman numerals.

16	XVI
163	CLXIII
205	CCV
13,523	MMMMMMMMMMMMMDXXIII

Content Note

Number vs. Numeral. It is mathematically correct to refer to **Roman numerals** and Hindu-Arabic numerals as numbers. A **numeral** is a symbol used to represent the abstract idea of a number. We often use the more familiar word "number" for both numeral and number. However, you may wish to discuss briefly with students that they will hear both terms and that either is acceptable.

Roman Numerals

One day, Mrs. Dewey started math class by asking, "How many of you speak another language besides English?"

> I speak Spanish.

> I speak Chinese.

> I speak Russian.

Many hands went up. Roberto and Ana speak Spanish, Ming speaks Chinese, and Nila speaks Arabic. Linda speaks Tagalog, a language spoken in the Philippines, and Nicholas speaks Russian.

"That's wonderful," said Mrs. Dewey. "Did you know that there are over 220 major languages in the world? Many cultures have their own language, but almost all share the same number system. They use the digits 0, 1, 2, 3, 4, 5, 6, 7, 8, 9 to count and compute."

The number system we and many other people use is called the Hindu-Arabic number system. It was invented around the 9th century A.D. Many cultures had invented number systems well before this. One that is still used sometimes in our culture is the **Roman numeral** system. You can sometimes find Roman numerals on clocks and on buildings and in movies. Sometimes the pages in the preface of a book are numbered using Roman numerals. Often, when people want to be a little bit fancy, they use Roman numerals. For example, the Super Bowls of the National Football League are all designated with Roman numerals.

The Romans used a system that was based on counting groups similar to ours. Romans didn't only make groups of ten, they also made groups of five. Archaeologists have found evidence that their system was being used around 260 BCE. No one is really certain about where the Roman symbols for the numerals came from. They may have come from finger counting used in the market or the tally marks used to keep track of things like farm animals and soldiers. Some of the modern Roman numerals we use now came from the words Romans used.

64   SG · Grade 4 · Unit 3 · Lesson 2   **Roman Numerals**

Student Guide - Page 64

Roman Numerals and Symbols

Early Roman Numerals	Modern Roman Numerals	Hindu-Arabic Numbers	Possible Origins	
			Finger Counting or Latin Words	Tally Marks
I	I	1		I
V	V	5		V
X	X	10		X
	L	50		
C	C	100	The Latin word for one hundred is *centum*	(X)
Ɔ	D	500		
Φ	M	1000	The Latin word for one thousand is *mille*	<I>

To write a number like 123, Romans put together their symbols for one hundred, two tens, and three ones to write the number like this:

CXXIII

At first, the Romans just used the symbols for ones, tens, hundreds, and thousands. So a number like 876 might have looked like this:

CCCCCCCCXXXXXXXIIIIII

To help make these numbers shorter, Romans began using symbols for half of ten, half of one hundred, and half of one thousand. Then, they could write 876 as:

DCCCLXXVI

Roman Numerals   SG · Grade 4 · Unit 3 · Lesson 2   65

Student Guide - Page 65

Content Note

Modern Roman Numerals. The evolution of the present day symbols known as Roman numerals is long and complicated. The Roman numerals used in modern times are quite different from those used by early Romans. Early numbers were closer to actual representations of tallying. During the middle ages, the Roman system of numerals was still commonly used, while the Hindu-Arabic system was growing in popularity. In third grade, students read the Adventure Book *Leonardo the Blockhead* which illustrates this gradual transition. During the period between the 8th century and the 1700s, the more modern Roman symbols for 100 (C) and 500 (D) became more standard.

There is no single explanation that accounts for the historical development of all the symbols we use today in writing Roman numerals. Some ideas of how these numerals developed are presented on the Roman Numerals and Symbols chart on the *Roman Numerals* Activity Pages in the *Student Guide.*

Possibly the I, V, and X may have come from the system of finger counting used in the marketplace. Other evidence supports the idea that numerals were developed from tally marks recorded on sticks by farmers and merchants to keep records. In the tally system if the I is crossed it produces X and half of ten is five or V.

It is not known how the symbol L came to mean fifty. It may have been part of the tally system or may have been borrowed from another culture. The symbols for 100 and 1000 became C and M because of the words being used to identify one hundred (centum) and one thousand (mille).

The Subtractive Principle. Today, when we write Roman numerals, we use a subtractive principle, where a symbol for a smaller unit is placed before a symbol for the next larger unit to indicate that the smaller should be subtracted from the larger. This principle follows certain rules in order to avoid confusion: I can only precede V or X. X can only precede L or C. C can only precede D or M.

For example, instead of writing XXXX as 40, write it as XL. By placing the X in front of the L, it means "subtract 10 from 50," XL = 40.

Short-cutting the notation in this way seems to be more commonly used after the 8th century. This was not a universal practice during the time of the Romans. Inscriptions and writings from the 1st century A.D. show the use of a cumulative notation similar to that used by the Egyptians (44 would have been written as XXXXIIII not as XLIV).

Although today we have developed standard practices for writing the numerals, during the time when these numerals were in everyday use, they were written in a variety of conventions. The subtractive principle was never universally used until recent times. Earlier Romans could express 437 as either: CCCCXXXIIIIIII or CDXXXVII.

Have students complete *Questions 1–3* on the *Roman Numerals* Activity Pages in the *Student Guide.* In *Question 3,* students study the patterns presented by the numerals 1–100 and in counting by ones and tens. Discuss with them the patterns and their ideas on how to explain the **subtractive principle** before presenting it formally.

1. Use the chart to help you write these Roman numerals as Hindu-Arabic numbers:
   A. LXXXVIII
   B. MDCCLXXVII
   C. MMMMMMMMCCL

2. Write the following Hindu-Arabic numbers as Roman numerals:
   A. 68
   B. 108
   C. 286

3. In the earliest Roman times, four was written as "IIII" and nine was written as "VIIII." Later, a shorter way of writing numbers was invented. Study the table below to find the pattern for the shortcut. Copy the tables, then fill in the empty boxes in the top and bottom rows.

A.

I	II	III	IV					IX	
1	2	3		5	6	7	8		10

B.

	XII			XV		XVII		XIX	
11	12	13	14	15	16	17	18		20

C.

X	XX		XL		LX	LXX		XC	C
10	20	30		50			80		100

D. What patterns did you find?
E. Can you give a rule for the shortcuts in the table?

This pattern or rule is called the **subtractive principle.** The symbol for a smaller number is placed before a symbol for the larger number to indicate that the smaller number should be subtracted from the larger. **I** can only come in front of the **V** or **X**. **X** can only be subtracted from **L** or **C**. **C** can only be subtracted from **D** or **M**.

Student Guide - Page 66

Question 4 presents examples of the subtractive principle. Make sure students understand that when they see a Roman numeral with smaller numbers to the left of larger ones, the smaller number is meant to be subtracted from the larger.

For *Question 5*, help students to identify how numbers can be written in more than one way. For example: *Question 5A* can be answered with either LIIII or LIV, *Question 5B* can be answered with XXXXIIIIIII or XLVII, *Question 5C* can be answered with CLXXXXII or CXCII, and *Question 5D* can be answered with MDCCCCLXXXXIIIIII or MCMXCVI. Students will probably be able to think of more variations by combining different ways to write each part of the number. Point out that the modern system favors the shortest version.

In *Question 6*, Ana realizes that the Romans did not have the number 0.

Today, Roman numerals are rarely used to show numbers beyond the thousands. They are used primarily for emphasis or to represent numerals with more formality or importance. The ten digits of the Hindu-Arabic system allow us to write much larger numbers more efficiently.

Content Note

Zero. As with the Egyptians, Romans had no symbol for zero. In the Hindu-Arabic system, when we write 430, we know the 3 is three tens since it occupies the second position from the right. The zero shows us that there are no ones. Romans used an X to represent each ten and then used three Xs to show thirty.

Suggestions for Teaching the Lesson

Homework and Practice

• Ask students to bring examples of Roman numerals that they can find at home.

• Have students translate Hindu-Arabic numbers into Roman numerals or Roman numerals into Hindu-Arabic numbers by writing several on the board for students to copy. Super Bowl numbers and dates make interesting problems.

• Assign the problems in the Homework section on the *Roman Numerals* Activity Pages in the *Student Guide.*

---

4. Use this pattern to write the Hindu-Arabic numbers for the following Roman numerals.
   A. XXXIV
   B. XLIV
   C. CMXCIX
   D. MCMXLVIII

5. Write the Roman numerals for the following Hindu-Arabic numbers in more than one way.
   A. 54
   B. 47
   C. 192
   D. 1996

6. Ana said, "I can think of one number we can't write in Roman numerals." What number is Ana thinking about?

7. Where do you see Roman numerals today?

Homework

Dear Family Member:

Your child is learning how to translate our numbers (Hindu-Arabic) into Roman numerals. Ask your child about Roman numerals that he or she may have seen. Then, help your child with the translations. Encourage your child to use the Roman Numerals and Symbols chart as a guide.

Thank you for your cooperation.

1. Write these numbers using Roman numerals.
   A. 12
   B. 74
   C. 126
   D. 239

2. Write these Roman numerals as Hindu-Arabic numbers.
   A. XIV
   B. DXLV
   C. DCCXXIII
   D. CMXCVIII

Roman Numerals   SG · Grade 4 · Unit 3 · Lesson 2   67

Student Guide - Page 67

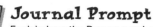

Journal Prompt

Explain how the Roman number system is different from our number system.

Suggestions for Teaching the Lesson (continued)

Assessment

Use the Journal Prompt to gain insight into students' understanding of the Roman and the Hindu-Arabic number systems.

Extension

- Children can develop their own base-ten number system. If students need help getting started, suggest they create symbols for 1, 10, 100, etc. Alternatively, they may create new symbols for the digits 0–9. Have them translate several Hindu-Arabic numbers into their new system.

- Students can develop their own number systems that are not based on 10.

Literature Connections

- Burns, Marilyn. *The I Hate Mathematics Book.* Little, Brown, and Company, Boston, MA, 1976.

- Haskins, Jim. *Count Your Way through the Arab World,* illustrated by Dana Gustafson. Scott Foresman, Glenview, IL, 1988.

- Ifrah, Georges. *The Universal History of Numbers: From Prehistory to the Invention of the Computer.* John Wiley & Sons, Hoboken, NJ, 2000.

- Schmandt-Besserat, Denise. *The History of Counting.* Morrow Junior, New York, NY, 1999.

- St. John, Glory. *How to Count Like a Martian.* Hill & Wang Publishing, New York, NY, 1975.

Resources

- Menninger, Karl. *Number Words and Number Symbols: A Cultural History of Numbers.* Dover Publications, Inc., New York, NY, 1992.

- Eves, Howard. *An Introduction to the History of Mathematics.* Harcourt Brace College Publishers, New York, NY, 1990.

AT A GLANCE

Developing the Activity

1. Students read the *Roman Numerals* Activity Pages in the *Student Guide.*

2. Students practice reading and writing Roman numerals.

3. Discuss *Questions 1–7* on the *Roman Numerals* Activity Pages.

Homework

Assign the Homework section on the *Roman Numerals* Activity Pages.

Assessment

Use the Journal Prompt to assess students' understanding of how the Roman and the Hindu-Arabic systems compare.

Notes:

Student Guide

Questions 1–7 (SG pp. 66–67)

I. **A.** 88

B. 1777

C. 8250

2. **A.** LXVIII

B. CVIII

C. CCLXXXVI

3. **A.**

I	II	III	IV	V	VI	VII	VIII	IX	X
1	2	3	4	5	6	7	8	9	10

B.

XI	XII	XIII	XIV	XV	XVI	XVII	XVIII	XIX	XX
11	12	13	14	15	16	17	18	19	20

C.

X	XX	XXX	XL	L	LX	LXX	LXXX	XC	C
10	20	30	40	50	60	70	80	90	100

D. *Answers will vary. One possible solution may be that after three repeats of a symbol, it changes to the subtractive principle.

E. *Answers will vary. All the fours and the nines are shown using the subtractive principle.

4. **A.** 34

B. 44

C. 999

D. 1948

5. **A.** *LIV or LIIII

B. *XLVII or XXXXVII

C. *CXCII or CLXXXXII

D. *MCMXCVI or MDCCCCLXXXXVI

6. *0

7. Answers will vary. On books, buildings, clocks, Super Bowls, etc.

Homework (SG p. 67)

Questions 1–2

I. **A.** XII

B. LXXIV or LXXIIII

C. CXXVI

D. CCXXXIX or CCXXXVIIII

2. **A.** 14

B. 545

C. 723

D. 998

*Answers and/or discussion are included in the Lesson Guide.

**Answers for all the Home Practice in the *Discovery Assignment Book* are at the end of the unit.

LESSON GUIDE 3
Place Value

 Students work with connecting cubes to review grouping by tens and ones and the use of base-ten pieces. While all students need to have the concept reinforced, some teachers may find their students can move quickly through this section or move directly to the next lesson. An assessment page is provided to help determine students' level of understanding.

Key Content

• Understanding place value: tens and ones.

• Grouping and counting by tens and ones.

• Translating between different representations of numbers (concrete, pictorial, symbolic).

• Representing 2-digit numbers with base-ten pieces.

Key Vocabulary

base-ten pieces
bits
Fewest Pieces Rule
place value
skinnies

OPTIONAL LESSON

> **There are no Daily Practice and Problems items for this lesson.**

Curriculum Sequence

Before This Unit

Place Value. Students used base-ten pieces to study place value and grouping in Grade 3 Units 4 and 6. These units introduced the TIMS Candy Company as a context for studying place value with base-ten pieces.

After This Unit

Place Value. Place-value concepts are explored further in Lesson 4. Larger numbers (up into the millions) are explored in Unit 6 and in Grade 5 Unit 2.

Materials List

Print Materials for Students

	Optional Activity	Written Assessment
Unit Resource Guide		*Working with Base-Ten Pieces* Page 44, 1 per student (optional)
Generic Section ⊙	*Base-Ten Board Part 1,* 1 per student and *Recording Sheet,* 1 per student plus extras	

⊙ *available on Teacher Resource CD*

All Transparency Masters, Blackline Masters, and Assessment Blackline Masters in the Unit Resource Guide are on the Teacher Resource CD.

Supplies for Each Student Pair

70 connecting cubes
base-ten pieces, if using the assessment (14 flats, 30 skinnies, 50 bits)

Materials for the Teacher

Transparency of *Base-Ten Board Part 1* Blackline Master (Unit Resource Guide, Generic Section and Teacher Resource CD)

Transparency of *Recording Sheet* Blackline Master (Unit Resource Guide, Generic Section and Teacher Resource CD)

Observational Assessment Record (Unit Resource Guide, Pages 9–10 and Teacher Resource CD)

connecting cubes

Before the Activity

A brief review of the material in this lesson may suffice for your class. Use the *Working with Base-Ten Pieces* Assessment Blackline Master to determine the level of your students' understanding. Students who have not worked extensively with manipulatives to develop place-value concepts may need to spend some time on this activity. If your students are new to base-ten pieces, place the pieces in a learning center about a week before the activity so that children have a chance to become familiar with them.

For *Question 1* on the *Working with Base-Ten Pieces* Assessment Blackline Master, most students will use 4 tens and 2 units. Other answers are correct. For example, if you see 3 tens and 12 units, ask the child if he or she can show you 42 in a different way, using fewer blocks. If the children are unable to show 42 using the fewest blocks, this lesson should be done thoroughly.

In *Question 2*, a student who understands place value should respond with 40 or 4 tens. The 4 is in the tens' place. In *Question 3*, Sam is correct in that 152 is represented, but he did not represent 152 in the most efficient manner. Sam can use fewer pieces by using 1 hundred, 5 tens, and 2 units. In *Question 4*, Ana is correct. Ana is regrouping. The 1 means one group of ten.

This assessment should give you an understanding of your students' knowledge of place value. Proceed with the activities accordingly. Understanding of whole number place value will be crucial to understanding decimals.

Developing the Activity

The context of the lesson is the TIMS Candy Company, an imaginary company that produces Chocos. To begin the activity, use the connecting cubes and the *Base-Ten Board Part 1*. The *Base-Ten Board* is used to keep track of how much candy has been made. Each individual Choco is represented by a **bit** (an individual cube). Bits can only be placed in the right-most column of the *Base-Ten Board* (the bits' column). Whenever there are ten bits, they can be packed (snapped) together to make a **skinny.** Skinnies are always placed in the skinnies' column. See Figure 3.

Distribute the connecting cubes and copies of the *Base-Ten Board Part 1* and *Recording Sheet*. Explain the TIMS Candy Company and the *Base-Ten Board* to the class. The *Recording Sheet* has columns for bits, skinnies, flats, and packs. Tell students that in this lesson they will only use the bits' and skinnies' columns. Show the *Base-Ten Board* on the overhead projector, magnetic board, or table so all can see and

TIMS Tip

The *Base-Ten Board* is used as a mat for the manipulatives. Students will use their *Base-Ten Boards* in subsequent lessons. The *Recording Sheet* is used to write the numbers represented by the base-ten pieces.

Base-Ten Board

Skinnies	Bits
▭	▯

Recording Sheet

			16

Figure 3: *16 bits on the* Base-Ten Board

Base-Ten Board

Skinnies	Bits
▭	▯
▭	▯ ▯
	▯ ▯
	▯ ▯

Recording Sheet

		1	6

Figure 4: *One skinny and six bits on the* Base-Ten Board

ask the class to count out 16 cubes. Illustrate that these 16 pieces are 16 bits so they must be placed in the bits' column. On the *Recording Sheet*, write 16 in the bits' column. This is shown in Figure 3.

Ask:

*   *Can any of these bits be packed? How?* (Ten cubes can be snapped together to form a skinny. Illustrate by snapping ten cubes together and placing the resulting skinny in the skinnies' column. This leaves six cubes in the bits' column.)
*   *How much candy has been made?* (One skinny and six bits. This should be recorded on the *Recording Sheet* as shown in Figure 4.)
*   *Is there more or less candy now than before we made the skinny?* (Students should realize that Figure 3 and Figure 4 represent the same amount of candy.)

Now use a larger number of bits and repeat the exercise above. For example, begin with 34 bits. Students should first record that there are 34 bits. They then make one skinny, leaving 24 bits. After snapping together another ten cubes and moving the skinny over to the next column, record two skinnies and 14 bits. There are enough bits left to make one more skinny. Thus, there are three skinnies and four bits. It often helps students to draw lines between the entries on the *Recording Sheet* as shown in Figure 5.

Recording Sheet

			34
		1	24
		2	14
		3	4

Figure 5: *Writing multiple entries on the* Recording Sheet

Students who used *Math Trailblazers* in third grade have worked with place value extensively before. If you feel your students are ready to move on, skip to the next paragraph. For students who need more work, repeat the activity for several more numbers, for example, 23, 38, and 41. For each number, have students count out the cubes on the board. They should then snap the cubes together in groups of ten and record their answers as they make the skinnies.

On the overhead *Recording Sheet* or blackboard, write 56 in the bits' column and ask:

- *How many skinnies can you make with 56 bits and how many bits will be left over?* (56 bits makes 5 skinnies with 6 bits left over)

Explain to the class that the different ways of recording 56 bits are all acceptable. The same amount of candy is represented if we write 56 as 3 skinnies and 26 bits or as 5 skinnies and 6 bits. However, we usually want to write our amounts using the fewest number of pieces. That is, we want to have fewer than ten pieces in each column. We refer to this idea as the **Fewest Pieces Rule.** (This rule was introduced in Grade 3.) Practice rewriting numbers as different combinations of skinnies and bits. It is crucial to understand how numbers can be represented in different forms to understand regrouping.

For example, place 3 skinnies and 17 bits on the *Base-Ten Board* in the appropriate columns. Ask:

- *How else can this amount be arranged? Record your work on the* Recording Sheet.
- *Which way uses the Fewest Pieces Rule?*

Circle the representation that uses the Fewest Pieces Rule. Students should realize that this amount can be written and shown as:

`
     1 skinny, 37 bits
     2 skinnies, 27 bits
     3 skinnies, 17 bits
     4 skinnies, 7 bits (This representation uses
                  the Fewest Pieces Rule.)

Do more of these as needed.

Place 7 skinnies and 6 bits on the *Base-Ten Board*. Ask:

- *How many pieces of candy were made?* (76)

Do more examples of these as needed.

TIMS Tip

It is important that students enter their work on the *Recording Sheets*. This helps connect the concrete representation (the base-ten pieces) with the symbolic marks on paper.

Suggestions for Teaching the Lesson

Assessment

- Use the *Working with Base-Ten Pieces* Assessment Blackline Master to determine your students' current knowledge of place-value concepts. See Before the Activity.

- At the end of the activity, students should be able to:

  1. Represent a 2-digit number on the *Base-Ten Board* in a variety of ways using tens and ones.

  2. Represent a 2-digit number on the *Base-Ten Board* using the fewest pieces.

  3. Identify if a representation of a number on the *Base-Ten Board* is correct.

  4. Translate freely between the *Base-Ten Board* and the *Recording Sheet*.

As students work on examples, circulate through the room to assess their abilities. Make notes on the *Observational Assessment Record*.

Extension

The exercises described in the lesson can be turned into games.

1. One team lays out base-ten pieces on the *Base-Ten Board* (or just on a desk). A second team must translate these pieces into numbers on the *Recording Sheet*.

2. Same as above but the translation must use the Fewest Pieces Rule.

3. One team writes a number on the *Recording Sheet*. The other team must translate it to base-ten pieces on the *Base-Ten Board*.

4. Same as above but the team must provide at least two ways of representing the number on the *Base-Ten Board*.

AT A GLANCE

Developing the Activity

1. Use the *Working with Base-Ten Pieces* Assessment Blackline Master to determine your students' knowledge of place-value concepts. See Before the Activity.
2. Describe the context of the lesson, the TIMS Candy Company.
3. Introduce the connecting cubes as base-ten bits and skinnies.
4. Introduce the *Base-Ten Board* and the *Recording Sheet*.
5. Using the *Base-Ten Board,* students represent numbers using individual cubes. Then, they form groups of ten cubes by snapping individual cubes together. They record on the *Recording Sheet* the numbers represented with the cubes.
6. Students represent the same number in different ways on the *Base-Ten Board.* Students record the numbers on the *Recording Sheet.*
7. Discuss the Fewest Pieces Rule.
8. Students express a number in different ways on the *Base-Ten Board* and on the *Recording Sheet.* They identify which representation uses the Fewest Pieces Rule.

Assessment

1. Use the *Working with Base-Ten Pieces* Assessment Blackline Master to provide base-line information.
2. Use the *Observational Assessment Record* to document students' abilities to use base-ten pieces to represent two-digit numbers.

Notes:

Working with Base-Ten Pieces

Use a separate sheet of paper to record your answers to Questions 2–4.

1. Show the number 42 using the base-ten pieces. Your teacher will check your work.

2. What is the value of the 4 in the number 42? How do you know?

3. Here is a picture of how Sam showed the number 152 using the base-ten pieces.

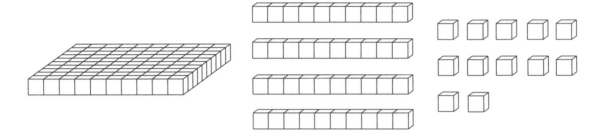

   A. Is Sam correct? Why or why not?

   B. Can you use fewer pieces than Sam? If so, show how.

4. Ana solved the problem 47 + 24 like this:

$$\overset{1}{4}7$$
$$+\ 24$$
$$\overline{71}$$

   Is she correct? Why did she write a 1 above the 47?

Unit Resource Guide

Working with Base-Ten Pieces (URG p. 44)

Questions 1–4

1. *Answers will vary. One possible solution is shown.

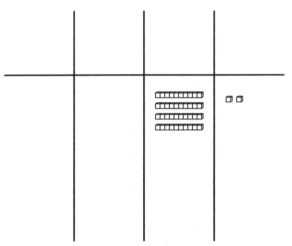

2. *40; Answers will vary. The four stands for four tens or four skinnies. Four skinnies have a value of 40.

3. **A.** *Yes; Answers will vary. The sum of all the base-ten pieces is 152.

   B. *Yes.

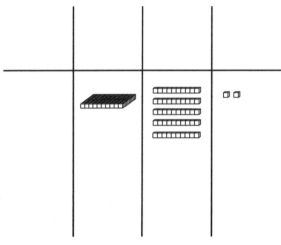

4. *Ana is correct. Ana added 7 ones and 4 ones. She got 11 ones or 1 ten and 1 one. She recorded the 1 one in the ones' place. She carried the 1 ten to the tens' place.

*Answers and/or discussion are included in the Lesson Guide.
**Answers for all the Home Practice in the *Discovery Assignment Book* are at the end of the unit.

LESSON GUIDE

The TIMS Candy Company

Estimated Class Sessions: 1–2

Students use base-ten pieces to keep track of how much candy is made at the TIMS Candy Company. The hundreds and thousands places are reviewed. Students practice trading pieces and expressing equivalent amounts in different ways. Base-ten shorthand is reviewed to help students develop pictorial representations of the base-ten system, with the goal of bridging concrete and symbolic representations.

Key Content

- Understanding place value: hundreds and thousands.
- Representing large numbers using base-ten pieces.
- Translating between different representations of numbers (concrete, pictorial, symbolic).
- Developing number sense for large numbers.

Key Vocabulary

base-ten pieces
base-ten shorthand
bits
Fewest Pieces Rule
flats
packs
place value
skinnies

Materials List

Print Materials for Students

		Math Facts and Daily Practice and Problems	Activity	Homework
Student Books	**Student Guide**		*The TIMS Candy Company* Pages 68–76	*The TIMS Candy Company* Homework Section Page 77
	Discovery Assignment Book			Home Practice Part 5 Page 26
Teacher Resources	**Facts Resource Guide** ⊙	DPP Items 3E & 3F		
	Unit Resource Guide	DPP Items E–F Page 15 ⊙	*Base-Ten Pieces* Blackline Masters Pages 55–56, 2 per student pair of the bits and skinnies master and 3 of the flats and packs master (optional)	
	Generic Section ⊙		*Base-Ten Board Parts 1 and 2,* 1 per student pair and *Recording Sheet,* 1 per student plus extras	

⊙ *available on Teacher Resource CD*

All Transparency Masters, Blackline Masters, and Assessment Blackline Masters in the Unit Resource Guide are on the Teacher Resource CD.

Supplies for Each Student Pair

set of base-ten pieces—2 packs, 14 flats, 30 skinnies (rods), 50 bits (units)

Materials for the Teacher

Transparency of *Recording Sheet* Blackline Master (Unit Resource Guide, Generic Section and Teacher Resource CD), optional

Observational Assessment Record (Unit Resource Guide, Pages 9–10 and Teacher Resource CD)

overhead base-ten pieces, optional

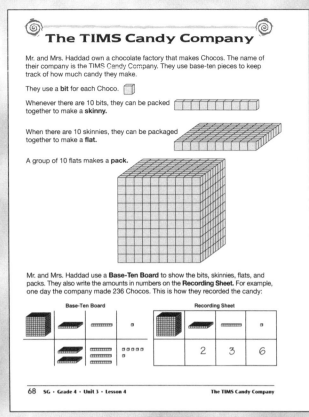

Student Guide - Page 68

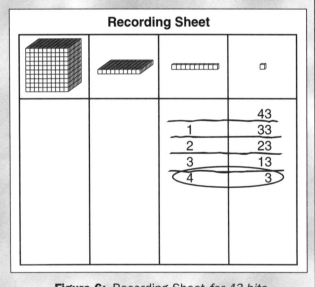

Figure 6: Recording Sheet *for 43 bits*

TIMS Tip

It is not practical because of size limitations to have an overhead transparency of the *Base-Ten Board* with all four columns. If you are using an overhead and are working with flats and packs, explain the difficulty to the class. Then either lay the pieces on the overhead, however they fit, or switch to a magnetic board or a table for illustration purposes. Sketch the *Recording Sheet* on the blackboard.

Before the Activity

If you chose to omit Lesson 3, be sure to review the following terms at the appropriate time:

- The *Base-Ten Board Parts 1* and *2* is a mat where the manipulatives (connecting cubes or base-ten pieces) are placed.
- The *Recording Sheet* is where numbers are recorded in writing.
- Individual cubes are called **bits.** When 10 bits are snapped together, they form a **skinny.**
- The **Fewest Pieces Rule** refers to the idea that we often want to represent quantities using the fewest number of base-ten pieces possible, i.e., using fewer than 10 pieces in any place-value column.

See the Background and Lesson Guide 3 for a more thorough explanation of the terms. Also see the TIMS Tutor: *Arithmetic* in the *Teacher Implementation Guide.*

TIMS Tip

Use resealable plastic bags, shoe boxes, or plastic storage boxes to store the sets of base-ten pieces. Pieces not in use should be kept in the containers.

Developing the Activity

Hand out base-ten pieces, *Recording Sheets,* and *Base-Ten Board Parts 1* and *2*. You may go through the material quickly if your class has previously worked with base-ten pieces. However, most students benefit from a review. If students hesitate when trading with the base-ten pieces, use connecting cubes to remind them of the idea that a skinny is ten cubes snapped together. Explain to the class that it became tedious to snap cubes together, so the TIMS Candy Company came up with a more efficient set of blocks. The new blocks include ten bits that are already snapped together. Whenever they have ten **bits,** they can trade them for a **skinny.** The rules are the same: bits must stay in the bits' column and skinnies in the skinnies' column. When needed, they can also trade a skinny for ten bits.

Each group takes a handful of unit cubes (bits) and pretends this represents the number of Chocos they made at the TIMS Candy Company. They place the cubes on the *Base-Ten Board.* By making appropriate trades and recording each trade on the *Recording Sheets,* students express their amount of candy using the Fewest Pieces Rule. As in Lesson 3, separate the various representations by lines and identify the representation that uses the Fewest Pieces Rule. For example, Figure 6 shows how 43 bits can be recorded on the *Recording Sheet.* This activity should be repeated with different numbers until all students are proficient.

Explain to the class that in order for the TIMS Candy Company to operate as efficiently as possible, it decided that ten skinnies should form a new group called a **flat.** Place ten skinnies side-by-side to show this group is exactly the same size as a flat. Ask:

- *How many bits are in a flat?*

Have students skip count by tens to 100. When they have 10 skinnies, these can be exchanged for a flat and vice versa. Show them 3 flats and ask:

- *How many skinnies would there be if the flats were broken up?* (3 flats is the same as 30 skinnies or 300 bits.)

Do several more examples like this as needed.

Show 2 flats, 6 skinnies, and 4 bits. Ask:

- *How many bits would there be if the flats and skinnies were broken up and they were all in the bits' column?* (264 bits)

- *How else could 264 be shown or represented?*

Two possible answers are:

1 flat, 16 skinnies, 4 bits

and

1 flat, 15 skinnies, 14 bits

Once the class is familiar with the flats, introduce the **packs** as 10 flats. Make a pack together with the class as you stack flats atop one another. Have students count with you by 100s to 1000 to determine how many bits there are in a pack. Students should see the layers of flats that make a pack, otherwise they may think there are 600 bits in a pack (100 for each side of the cube rather than 100 for each layer). Repeat the stacking process and count how many skinnies there are in a pack, skip counting by tens. Note to the class that they can trade 10 flats for a pack and vice versa. To work with these larger amounts, use all four columns of the *Base-Ten Board Parts 1* and *2*.

Practice trading with the class by asking them to express amounts using the **Fewest Pieces Rule.**

Give the students the examples below and have them practice trading by placing the correct number of base-ten pieces on their *Base-Ten Boards.* They should continue trading until they have expressed the amount using the fewest number of pieces and record their work on their *Recording Sheets.*

1. 4 bits, 15 skinnies, 11 flats, 1 pack
2. 12 bits, 11 skinnies, 11 flats
3. 21 bits, 11 skinnies, 3 flats

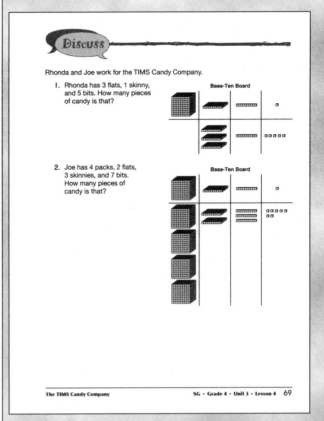

Student Guide - Page 69

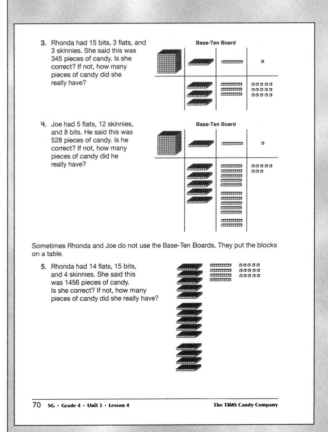

Student Guide - Page 70

Student Guide - Page 71

6. Joe had 2 packs, 5 skinnies, 4 flats, and 3 bits. He said this was 2543 pieces of candy. Is he correct? If not, how many pieces of candy did he really have?

Base-Ten Shorthand

Sometimes it is useful to record your work with the base-ten pieces. Other times, base-ten pieces are not available but drawing a picture of the base-ten pieces is helpful. Mr. Haddad decided to use a shorthand for the base-ten pieces.

• = Bit   / = Skinny   ⬜ = Flat   ⬜ = Pack

7. Joe says there are often several ways to show an amount of candy on the Base-Ten Board. For example, 26 can be shown as:

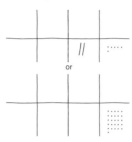

or

There is one more way 26 can be shown on the Base-Ten Board. What is this third way? Use base-ten shorthand to sketch your answer.

Student Guide - Page 71

Student Guide - Page 72

8. Use base-ten shorthand to show the number of candies Rhonda and Joe had in Questions 1–6.

9. Joe showed several ways of putting 32 Chocos on the Base-Ten Board by using base-ten shorthand. Some of Joe's work was erased. Fill in the missing pieces. Use base-ten shorthand to sketch your answer.

   A. Here is one way to show 32.

   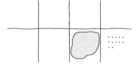

   B. Here is another way to show 32.

   C. Here is a third way to show 32.

Student Guide - Page 72

Figure 7 shows the trades on a *Recording Sheet* for Example 1: 4 bits, 15 skinnies, 11 flats, 1 pack.

Recording Sheet

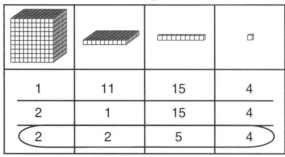

1	11	15	4
2	1	15	4
2	2	5	4

Figure 7: *Using the Fewest Pieces Rule*

Using the *Recording Sheets,* we keep the column markings when recording numbers. Children should realize that if there is only one digit in each column, then the column markings are not necessary. We know that the right-most column records bits, the next column records skinnies, etc. Problems arise only if we are not using the Fewest Pieces Rule. For example, if we have 4 flats, 12 skinnies, and 35 bits, we cannot write 41235 without column marks. Thus, the way we record numbers is a convention where we assume there is one digit in each column and each column is a place with a certain value attached.

Write a number, such as 376, on the board or overhead. Ask:

- *How many candies is this?*
- *How many candies does the 7 represent?* (70)
- *How many candies does the 3 represent?* (300)
- *How many candies does the 6 represent?* (6)

Thus 376 is 300 + 70 + 6 candies. Do several more of these as needed.

Introduce **base-ten shorthand.** Students who used the *Math Trailblazers* curriculum previously have already used the shorthand. Base-ten shorthand is a pictorial representation of the blocks; this is helpful as students move gradually from the concrete to the symbolic. It also provides a way to create a written record of students' work with the manipulatives. The shorthand is shown in Figure 8.

• = Bit   / = Skinny   ⬜ = Flat   ⬜ = Pack

Figure 8: *Base-ten shorthand*

Students can use base-ten shorthand to make a record of their work when they are asked to sketch the base-ten pieces. They can sketch a base-ten board as well when needed. The manipulatives, however, should not be abandoned. This is particularly important when introducing new concepts.

To practice base-ten shorthand, ask children to draw several numbers. Two examples are shown in Figure 9.

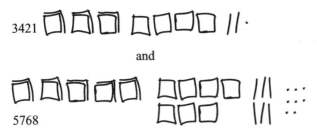

Figure 9: *Examples of base-ten shorthand*

Have students read *The TIMS Candy Company* Activity Pages in the *Student Guide* and complete the questions. The pages review the concepts discussed above and provide additional problems for students to solve.

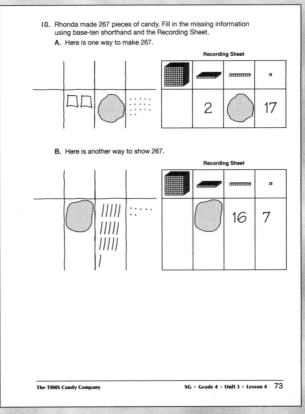

10. Rhonda made 267 pieces of candy. Fill in the missing information using base-ten shorthand and the Recording Sheet.
    A. Here is one way to make 267.

    B. Here is another way to show 267.

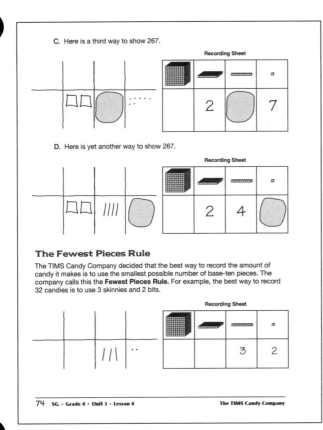

C. Here is a third way to show 267.

D. Here is yet another way to show 267.

The Fewest Pieces Rule

The TIMS Candy Company decided that the best way to record the amount of candy it makes is to use the smallest possible number of base-ten pieces. The company calls this the **Fewest Pieces Rule.** For example, the best way to record 32 candies is to use 3 skinnies and 2 bits.

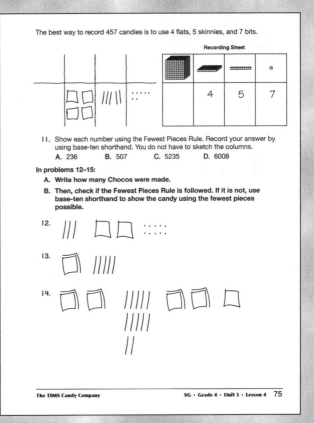

The best way to record 457 candies is to use 4 flats, 5 skinnies, and 7 bits.

11. Show each number using the Fewest Pieces Rule. Record your answer by using base-ten shorthand. You do not have to sketch the columns.
    A. 236   B. 507   C. 5235   D. 6008

In problems 12–15:
    A. Write how many Chocos were made.
    B. Then, check if the Fewest Pieces Rule is followed. If it is not, use base-ten shorthand to show the candy using the fewest pieces possible.

12.

13.

14.

Daily Practice and Problems: Task for Lesson 4

F. Task: Story Solving (URG p. 15)

A. Write a story to show 5 × 7. Draw a picture to go with your story. Write a number sentence on your picture.

B. Write a story and a number sentence to show 35 ÷ 7.

C. What are the other two facts in this fact family?

15.

Discuss _____

16. The number **157** has 3 digits: the 1, the 5, and the 7. Explain the value of each of the digits. Do you have the same amount if you mix up the digits and write **571**? Explain why or why not.

Student Guide - Page 76

Suggestions for Teaching the Lesson

Math Facts

- DPP Bit E provides practice skip counting by fives and tens in the context of time. Task F provides practice with fact families.

- Home Practice Part 5 provides practice with fact families.

Answers for Part 5 of the Home Practice can be found in the Answer Key at the end of this lesson and at the end of this unit.

Homework and Practice

The Homework section in the *Student Guide* provides valuable practice translating among concrete, pictorial, and symbolic representations of numbers.

Assessment

- Describe the following situation to the class:

  The class has a new student and you are assigned to work with him. To acquaint him with the base-ten pieces, show the number 2172 on the Base-Ten Board *and explain what each of the digits in the number means.*

- *Question 16* on *The TIMS Candy Company* Activity Pages can be used to assess understanding of place value concepts.

- Use the *Observational Assessment Record* to record students' abilities to represent numbers using base-ten pieces.

Homework

Dear Family Member:

Your child is reviewing place value—the idea that the value of a digit in a number depends upon where it is placed. For example, the 2 in 329 stands for 2 tens but the 2 in 7293 is 2 hundreds.

In class your child uses base-ten pieces to represent numbers. When the pieces are not available, students are encouraged to draw pictures of the base-ten pieces. We call these drawings of the base-ten pieces base-ten shorthand. To help your child with homework Questions 1–11, you may wish to review the Base-Ten Shorthand section on the previous pages.

Thank you for your cooperation.

The sketches below show the number of Chocos made by workers at the TIMS Candy Company. Write the amount of candy using numbers.

1. ||| ······

2. ☐ | ····

3. ☐☐ || ··

4. ☐☐

5. ☐ //////////

6. ☐☐ ·

The workers at the TIMS Candy Company recorded the amount of candy they made in numbers. Sketch each amount using base-ten shorthand.

7. 356
8. 4206
9. 240
10. 3005

11. One way to show 352 using base-ten shorthand is:

☐☐☐ //// :::::

Sketch 352 two other ways using base-ten shorthand.

The TIMS Candy Company   SG · Grade 4 · Unit 3 · Lesson 4   77

Student Guide - Page 77

Name _____ Date _____

Part 5 More Fact Families
Solve the problems below and complete the number sentences for the related facts.

A. $10 \times 10 =$ _____

_____ $\div 10 = 10$

B. $10 \div 5 =$ _____

_____ $\times 5 = 10$

$5 \times$ _____ = _____

_____ $\div$ _____ = 5

C. _____ $\div 10 = 3$

_____ $\div 3 =$ _____

$3 \times$ _____ = _____

_____ $\times 3 =$ _____

D. $6 \times$ _____ = 30

_____ $\times 6 =$ _____

$30 \div 6 =$ _____

$30 \div$ _____ = _____

E. $7 \times 10 =$ _____

_____ $\times 7 =$ _____

_____ $\div 7 =$ _____

_____ $\div$ _____ = _____

F. $1 \times 5 =$ _____

$5 \times$ _____ = _____

$5 \div$ _____ = _____

_____ $\div$ _____ = _____

26   DAB · Grade 4 · Unit 3   NUMBERS AND NUMBER OPERATIONS

Discovery Assignment Book - Page 26

AT A GLANCE

Math Facts and Daily Practice and Problems

DPP items E and F provide practice with the math facts for the fives and tens.

Developing the Activity

1. Introduce the base-ten pieces—bits and skinnies—as an efficient system for keeping track of the candy made by the TIMS Candy Company.
2. Students take a handful of bits. They make trades on a copy of *Base-Ten Board Part 1* and record each trade on the *Recording Sheet.*
3. Introduce the flat. Discuss how 10 skinnies can be exchanged for 1 flat and vice versa.
4. Represent a number using flats, skinnies, and bits. Students offer other ways of representing the same number. Repeat with other numbers.
5. Introduce the packs. Discuss how 10 flats can be exchanged for 1 pack and vice versa.
6. Students use the *Base-Ten Board Parts 1* and *2* to represent numbers using the Fewest Pieces Rule. They record their work on the *Recording Sheet* as well.
7. Discuss the need for columns.
8. Introduce base-ten shorthand.
9. Students draw several numbers using the shorthand.
10. Students read and discuss *The TIMS Candy Company* Activity Pages in the *Student Guide.* They complete *Questions 1–16.*

Homework

1. Assign students the homework on *The TIMS Candy Company* Activity Pages in the *Student Guide.*
2. Assign Part 5 of the Home Practice.

Assessment

Use the *Observational Assessment Record* to document students' abilities to represent numbers using base-ten pieces.

Notes:

Base-Ten Pieces

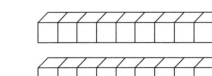

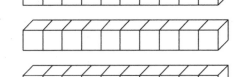

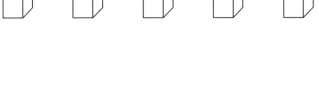

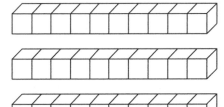

Base-Ten Pieces

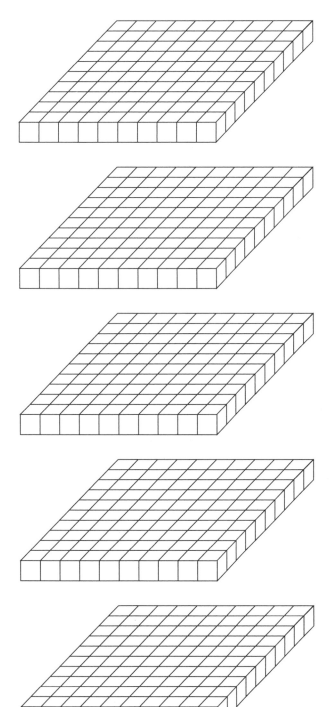

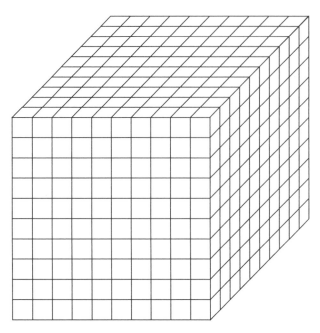

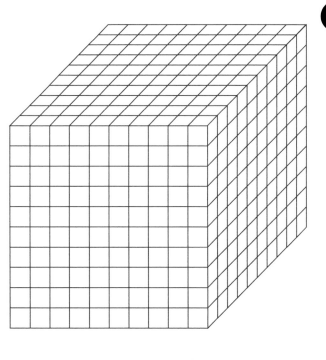

Student Guide

Questions 1–16 (SG pp. 69–76)

1. 315

2. 4237

3. Rhonda is correct.

4. Joe is incorrect. He has 628 pieces of candy.

5. Rhonda is incorrect. She has 1455 pieces of candy.

6. Joe is incorrect. He has 2453 pieces of candy.

7.

8. Answers will vary. Some possible solutions follow.

   1.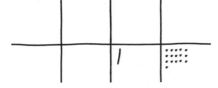

   2.

   3.

4.

5.

6.

9. A.

   B.

   C.

*Answers and/or discussion are included in the Lesson Guide.

**Answers for all the Home Practice in the *Discovery Assignment Book* are at the end of the unit.

10. **A.**

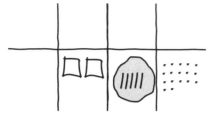

Recording Sheet

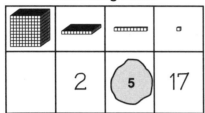

C.

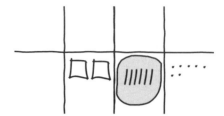

Recording Sheet

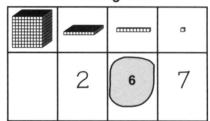

B.

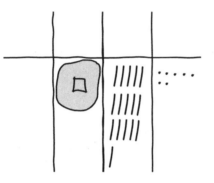

Recording Sheet

D.

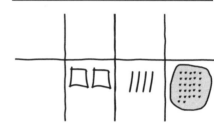

Recording Sheet

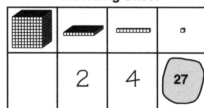

11. **A.**

B.

C.

*Answers and/or discussion are included in the Lesson Guide.
**Answers for all the Home Practice in the *Discovery Assignment Book* are at the end of the unit.

D.

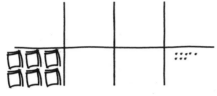

Homework (SG p. 77)

Questions 1–11

1. 37
2. 114
3. 2022
4. 1100
5. 1090
6. 2001
7.

12. **A.** 240
    B. No

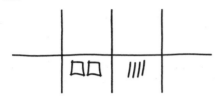

8.

13. **A.** 1050
    B. Yes
14. **A.** 4220
    B. No

9.

15. **A.** 4240
    B. No

10.

11.

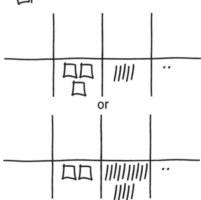

16. The 1 has a value of 100, the 5 has a value of 50, and the 7 has a value of 7. Mixing up the digits changes the value. If the digits were mixed up to be 571, the 5 would be worth 500, the 7 would be worth 70, and the 1 would be worth 1.

*Answers and/or discussion are included in the Lesson Guide.

**Answers for all the Home Practice in the *Discovery Assignment Book* are at the end of the unit.

Discovery Assignment Book

**Home Practice (DAB p. 26)

Part 5. More Fact Families

Questions A–F

A. $10 \times 10 = 100$
$100 \div 10 = 10$

B. $10 \div 5 = 2$
$2 \times 5 = 10$
$5 \times 2 = 10$
$10 \div 2 = 5$

C. $30 \div 10 = 3$
$30 \div 3 = 10$
$3 \times 10 = 30$
$10 \times 3 = 30$

D. $6 \times 5 = 30$
$5 \times 6 = 30$
$30 \div 6 = 5$
$30 \div 5 = 6$

E. $7 \times 10 = 70$
$10 \times 7 = 70$
$70 \div 7 = 10$
$70 \div 10 = 7$

F. $1 \times 5 = 5$
$5 \times 1 = 5$
$5 \div 5 = 1$
$5 \div 1 = 5$

*Answers and/or discussion are included in the Lesson Guide.
**Answers for all the Home Practice in the *Discovery Assignment Book* are at the end of the unit.

LESSON GUIDE 5

Addition and Subtraction

Estimated Class Sessions: 3

Students work with base-ten pieces to review place-value concepts and addition and subtraction procedures. Addition and subtraction of large numbers are practiced using the manipulatives. The standard addition and subtraction algorithms are used while solving addition and subtraction problems with the base-ten pieces. The standard algorithms are referred to as quick paper-and-pencil methods.

Key Content

- Understanding place value: hundreds and thousands.
- Representing addition and subtraction with base-ten pieces.
- Estimating sums and differences.

Daily Practice and Problems: Bits for Lesson 5

G. Play *Digits Game* Addition
(URG p. 16)

Draw boxes like these on your paper. As your teacher or classmate chooses the digits, place them in the boxes. Try to find the largest sum. Remember that each digit will be read only once.

□ □ □
+ □ □

I. Play *Digits Game* Subtraction
(URG p. 17)

Draw boxes like these on your paper. As your teacher or classmate chooses the digits, place them in the boxes. Try to find the largest difference. Remember that each digit will be read only once.

□ □ □
− □ □

K. Skip Counting (URG p. 18)

1. Start on 0 and skip count by 5s on the calculator for 15 seconds.

2. Start on 0 and skip count by 10s on the calculator for 15 seconds. How far did you get?

DPP Tasks are on page 70. Suggestions for using the DPPs are on page 70.

Curriculum Sequence

Before This Unit

Addition and Subtraction. Students used base-ten pieces and base-ten shorthand to represent addition and subtraction in Grade 3 Units 6 and 14.

After This Unit

Place Value. Students will use base-ten pieces to explore numbers into the millions in Unit 6. They will work with the pieces to explore multiplication in Unit 7. Students will encounter more practice with addition and subtraction in the Daily Practice and Problems, Home Practice, and the word problems in many units.

Materials List

Print Materials for Students

	Math Facts and Daily Practice and Problems	Activity	Homework	Written Assessment
Student Books — Student Guide		Addition and Subtraction Pages 78–84	Addition and Subtraction Homework Section Pages 84–85	
Student Books — Discovery Assignment Book			Home Practice Parts 2 & 3 Pages 23–24	
Teacher Resources — Facts Resource Guide ⊙	DPP Items 3H, 3K & 3L			
Teacher Resources — Unit Resource Guide ⊙	DPP Items G–L Pages 16–18			Place Value Addition and Subtraction Quiz Page 72, 1 per student
Teacher Resources — Generic Section ⊙		Base-Ten Pieces, 2 per student pair of the bits and skinnies master and 3 of the flats and packs master (optional), Base-Ten Board Parts 1 and 2, 1 of each per student pair, and Recording Sheet, 1 per student plus extras		

⊙   available on Teacher Resource CD

All Transparency Masters, Blackline Masters, and Assessment Blackline Masters in the Unit Resource Guide are on the Teacher Resource CD.

Supplies for Each Student Pair

set of base-ten pieces: 2 packs, 14 flats, 30 skinnies, 50 bits

Materials for the Teacher

Transparency of *Recording Sheet* Blackline Master (Unit Resource Guide, Generic Section and Teacher Resource CD)

Transparency of *Base-Ten Board Part 1* Blackline Master (Unit Resource Guide, Generic Section and Teacher Resource CD)

Observational Assessment Record (Unit Resource Guide, Pages 9–10 and Teacher Resource CD)

overhead base-ten pieces, optional

Developing the Activity

Part 1. Addition with Base-Ten Pieces

Hand out base-ten pieces and copies of the *Base-Ten Board Parts 1* and *2* and the *Recording Sheet*. Describe the following situation:

- *Rhonda and Joe both work for the TIMS Candy Company. In one hour, Rhonda made 36 pieces of candy. She packed these as 3 skinnies and 6 bits. Joe made 47 pieces of candy and he recorded his as 4 skinnies and 7 bits.*

Illustrate the problem with base-ten pieces using the *Base-Ten Board* transparency, a magnetic board, or a desk. Model the use of base-ten shorthand on the chalkboard as shown in Figure 10. Ask:

- *Altogether Rhonda and Joe have 7 skinnies and 13 bits. Could Rhonda and Joe record the candy they made together using fewer base-ten pieces?*

Since they now have 13 bits altogether, they can make one skinny and have 3 bits left over. Since one skinny is moved to the skinnies' column, they now have 8 skinnies and 3 bits. We can use the *Recording Sheet* to record the computation as shown in Figure 11.

Since most students have previously learned the standard addition algorithm, it can be tied in with their work with the base-ten pieces immediately. Point out to the class that when they add the 6 bits with the 7 bits they can regroup in their heads and think "that's 1 skinny and 3 bits." This can be directly translated to what we do when we write the 3 in the ones' column and write a 1 on top by the tens' column. The little "1" is the extra skinny we have formed. In the last step, we add our skinnies to get 8 skinnies. See Figure 12. Explain to the class that since they are skipping steps (or doing the problem in their heads) you can refer to this as the **quick paper-and-pencil method for addition.**

$$
\begin{array}{r}
3\overset{1}{6} \\
+\ 47 \\
\hline
83
\end{array}
$$

Figure 12: *Adding 36 and 47*

If you have students who have trouble using the standard algorithm, it may be helpful for them to do the addition problem as shown in Figure 13.

$$
\begin{array}{r}
36 \\
+\ 47 \\
\hline
13 \\
70 \\
\hline
83
\end{array}
$$

Figure 13: *Adding 36 and 47 with an extra step*

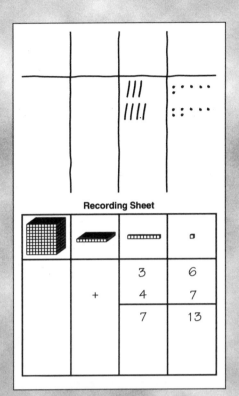

Figure 10: *Rhonda and Joe's first record*

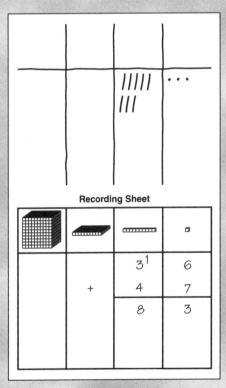

Figure 11: *Rhonda and Joe's second record*

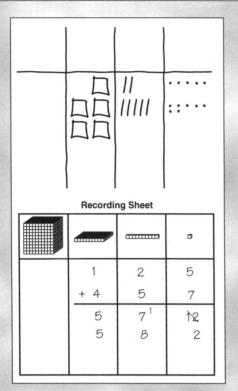

Figure 14: *Joe's 125 pieces plus Rhonda's 457 pieces*

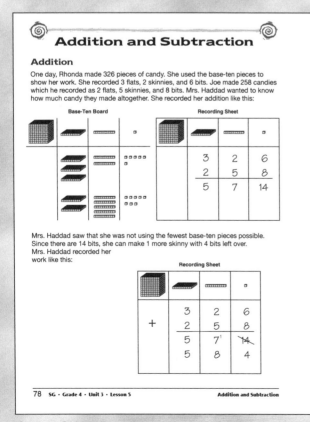

Student Guide - Page 78

The above activity should be repeated with several more examples in the context of combining candy. Use the following examples:

$$45 + 12$$
$$38 + 46$$

Students should model the situation on the *Base-Ten Board* and work the problem using an algorithm. Even students who are proficient with an algorithm can benefit from having the concept reinforced with the base-ten pieces.

In this lesson, the bit is designated as one unit. To bridge the base-ten pieces and the base-ten system, gradually begin referring to the bits as ones, the skinnies as tens, the flats as hundreds, and packs as thousands.

Pose a problem with more than two addends. Model the problem with base-ten pieces first; then do it using the quick paper-and-pencil method. For example:

- *Tom also works at the TIMS Candy Company. One day, Rhonda made 54 pieces of candy, Joe made 37, and Tom made 26. How much candy was made altogether?* (117)

- *On another day, Joe made 125 pieces of candy which he represented by 1 pack, 2 skinnies, and 5 bits. Rhonda packed 457 pieces of candy which she wrote as 4 packs, 5 skinnies, and 7 bits. How much candy did they pack altogether?* (582)

Students should do the problem using the base-ten pieces and then use paper and pencil. Students can also use base-ten shorthand. Remind the class that the total can be written as 5 packs, 7 skinnies, and 12 bits. However, we want to use the fewest number of pieces and have only one digit in each column. Thus, we trade 10 bits for 1 skinny, leaving 2 bits, and increase the skinnies to 8 as shown in Figure 14.

Repeat the problem above, but pretend Joe packed 185 pieces of candy. Set the problem up on the *Base-Ten Board* and record the numbers. See Figure 15.

Recording Sheet

pack	flat	skinny	bit
	1	8	5
	4	5	7
	5	1̶3̶	12
	5¹	3	1̶2̶
	6	3¹	2
	6	4	2

Figure 15: *Joe's 185 pieces plus Rhonda's 457 pieces*

This problem requires students to regroup twice, since the total number of pieces is 5 flats, 13 skinnies, and 12 bits. Students can trade 10 skinnies for a flat, leaving 6 flats, 3 skinnies, and 12 bits. The problem is completed by trading 10 bits for a skinny, leaving 6 flats, 4 skinnies, and 2 bits. Show students that it works as well to start with the bits' column and work to the left. Mention that with harder problems it may become confusing to begin working with the column to the left. To keep their work organized, it may be better to get in the habit of working from the right.

When appropriate, point out that the standard algorithm is often not the quickest, nor most efficient way to solve the problem. For example, ask:

- *Find different ways to add 2004 to 1876 without using the algorithm.*

Discuss strategies with students and encourage them to find different ways of doing the problem. One person might add the 4 to 1876 to get 1880 and then add 2000 to get 3880. Another person might add the 2000 first.

Picturing base-ten pieces is a good way for children to estimate. For example, pose the following problem:

- *There are 527 students at one school and 619 students at another school going on an outing. How many students are there from both schools?*

Ask students to imagine base-ten pieces representing the number of students at the schools. They should see that 527 is 5 flats (and some skinnies and bits) and 619 is 6 flats (and some skinnies and bits). Thus, the number of students altogether is about 11 flats (1 pack and 1 flat) or 1100 students.

This type of reasoning is often called **front-end estimation.** We estimate by using only the digits on the farthest left of a number. Thinking about base-ten pieces makes this easier because we think about the largest base-ten piece involved. Suggest more problems to solve using front-end estimation.

$$843 + 426 = \quad 134 + 234 = \quad 550 + 435 =$$

Then, ask:

- *Estimate the sum of 587 and 576 using front-end estimation.* (1000)
- *What is the exact answer?* (1163)
- *Is there a way we could have made a closer estimate?* (Using more appropriate convenient numbers instead of front-end, i.e., 600 + 600)

Read and discuss *Questions 1–3* of the *Addition and Subtraction* Activity Pages in the *Student Guide.* Students should then do *Questions 1–10* in the Homework section.

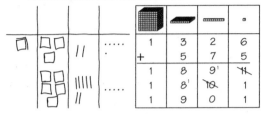

1. On another day, Rhonda made 1326 candies and Joe made 575. They recorded their work by sketching the base-ten pieces using base-ten shorthand. Use your base-ten pieces to solve this problem.

Joe remembered the Fewest Pieces Rule and wrote:

			o
1	3	2	6
+ 5	7	5
1	8	9¹	1̶1̶
1	8¹	1̶0̶	1
1	9	0	1

Mrs. Haddad noticed that drawing columns on the **Recording Sheet** was not necessary if she always used the Fewest Pieces Rule. Mrs. Haddad called this the **quick paper-and-pencil method for addition.** She wrote the problem like this:

$$
\begin{array}{r}
1\overset{1}{3}\overset{1}{2}6 \\
+\ 575 \\
\hline
1901
\end{array}
$$

At the end of one day Rhonda had made 1046, Joe had made 878, and Sam had made 767 candies. Mrs. Haddad found their total using the quick paper-and-pencil method:

$$
\begin{array}{r}
1\overset{1}{0}\overset{2}{4}6 \\
878 \\
+\ 767 \\
\hline
2691
\end{array}
$$

2. Explain Mrs. Haddad's method for adding the three numbers.

Student Guide - Page 79

3. Dominque has 325 baseball cards. Her sister Rosie has 416. About how many baseball cards do the two girls have altogether?

One way to estimate is to think about base-ten pieces. The number of baseball cards Dominque has is 3 flats and some more. The number of baseball cards Rosie has is 4 flats and some more. Together they have 7 flats and some more—or over 700 baseball cards.

I have about 300 baseball cards. You have about 400 baseball cards.

That means we have about 700 baseball cards.

Subtraction

Next to the factory, Mr. and Mrs. Haddad have a store where they sell their Chocos. They keep track of how much candy is sold using the base-ten pieces. Sometimes they have to break apart skinnies, flats, or packs to keep track of how much candy they have in the store.

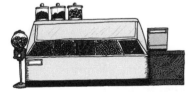

Student Guide - Page 80

Content Note

Subtraction on the *Base-Ten Board*. When modeling subtraction on the *Base-Ten Board*, the amount being taken away, the subtrahend, is not represented with the blocks. This is because this amount is being removed from the amount on the board. It is a common mistake for students to want to represent both the numbers in a subtraction problem on the *Base-Ten Board*.

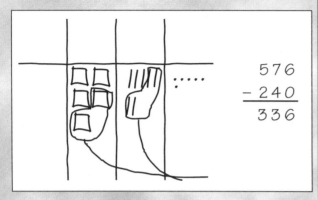

Figure 16: *576 – 240*

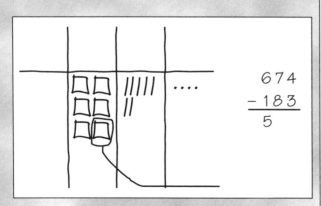

Figure 17: *674 – 183, first try*

Part 2. Subtraction with Base-Ten Pieces

To review the concept of subtraction, do the following problems together as a group using the base-ten pieces on the *Base-Ten Board* in the context of the story. As you work through the examples, ask students to estimate before doing the problems.

Example with No Regrouping: 576 – 240

- *The TIMS Candy Company has a store where it sells the chocolate it makes. Rhonda and Joe need to keep track of how much candy is in the store. One day, the store had 576 pieces of candy. That is, they had 5 flats, 7 skinnies, and 6 bits. A customer came in and bought 2 flats, 4 skinnies, and no bits (240 pieces of candy). How much candy was left after he made his purchase?*

Students should show 576 on the *Base-Ten Board* and then record 576 on a separate piece of paper. Since they sold 240 pieces of candy, we are subtracting 240 from 576. Students should physically remove 2 flats, 4 skinnies, and 0 bits from their boards leaving 3 flats, 3 skinnies, and 6 bits in the store. This is shown in Figure 16. Note that convention dictates that we begin at the right. However, it is intuitive to begin on the left. No harm is done if students do so. Work the problem using the standard algorithm (the quick paper-and-pencil method for subtraction) alongside the manipulatives. In the examples here, the use of the *Recording Sheet,* i.e., the use of labeled columns, has been eliminated. Use the *Recording Sheet* if you feel it would aid your students' understanding.

Here are more problems that do not involve regrouping:

$$468 - 51 \qquad 658 - 327$$
$$2416 - 402 \qquad 1206 - 402$$

Ask:

- *How could you do the last problem in your heads?* (Since 402 is 2 more than 400, the 400 can be subtracted from 1206 giving 806. Then, taking away 2 more leaves 804.)

Example with One Regrouping: 674 – 183

- *On another day, the store had 674 pieces of candy represented by 6 flats, 7 skinnies, and 4 bits. Another customer came in and bought 183 pieces of candy (1 flat, 8 skinnies, and 3 bits). How much candy will be left?* (491 pieces of candy)

As shown in Figure 17, many will first remove 1 flat and then try to remove 8 skinnies. However, there are only 7 skinnies available. The only solution is to break apart a flat. Make sure every child sees the problem here and physically takes a flat from the flats' column and exchanges it for 10 skinnies. Since skinnies only live in the skinnies' column, we now have 4 flats, 17 skinnies, and 4 bits. We can now take 8 skinnies away, leaving 9 skinnies. We finish the problem by taking 3 bits away, leaving 4 flats, 9 skinnies, and 1 bit in the store. See Figure 18.

Note that while working from the left works, we need to revisit the flats column. Rework the problem starting on the right.

Many students try to perform the subtraction algorithm without understanding. This leads to many errors, especially when regrouping more than once is involved. Students should do many examples using the base-ten blocks so that they develop a strong mental image of working with the blocks that will help them when the blocks are not available.

Some more problems involving one regrouping:

$$576 - 238 \qquad 2178 - 1422$$
$$607 - 532 \qquad 5364 - 219$$

Example with Two Regroupings: 3522 − 1248

* *The TIMS Candy Company had 3 packs, 5 flats, 2 skinnies, and 2 bits of candy. It sells 1 pack, 2 flats, 4 skinnies, and 8 bits. How many candies are left?*

Students place the base-ten pieces for 3522 on their boards and record the problem with numbers on a separate sheet of paper. Encourage students to start at the right. One solution is shown in Figures 19 and 20. Since 8 bits cannot be taken away from 2 bits, we break apart a skinny leaving 1 skinny and 12 bits. Then we can take 8 bits away, leaving 4 bits.

We cannot, however, subtract 4 skinnies from 1 skinny. To take 4 skinnies away, we must break apart a flat, leaving 3 packs, 4 flats, and 11 skinnies. We can then complete the problem leaving 2 packs, 2 flats, 7 skinnies, and 4 bits. See Figure 20.

Below are more examples. Students should use the base-ten pieces or base-ten shorthand as shown in Figures 19 and 20. Encourage students to estimate and to explain their thinking to each other.

$$501 - 199 \qquad 5628 - 1834$$
$$7124 - 985 \qquad 3003 - 1658$$

Problems that contain several zeros are often very difficult for students. Practice with the base-ten pieces alleviates these difficulties. Encourage students to use the base-ten pieces whenever they experience confusion with the algorithm. Later, sometimes just reminding them to think about the base-ten pieces is enough to help them proceed.

Figure 18: *674 − 183, second try*

Figure 19: *Break apart 1 skinny into 10 bits. Then, take away 8 bits.*

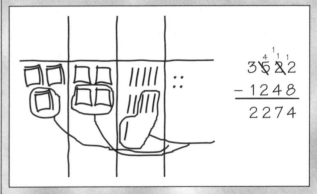

Figure 20: *Break apart 1 flat into 10 skinnies. Then, take away 4 skinnies, 2 flats, and 1 pack.*

Student Guide - Page 81

One morning, there were 3 flats, 6 skinnies, and 4 bits worth of candy in the store.

Base-Ten Board

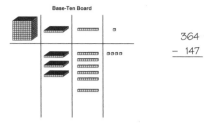

$$\begin{array}{r} 364 \\ -\ 147 \end{array}$$

A customer came in and bought 147 pieces of candy. To find how much candy was left, Mrs. Haddad did the following:

Since 7 bits cannot be taken away from 4 bits, a skinny must be broken apart. Then there are 3 flats, 5 skinnies, and 14 bits. Now 1 flat, 4 skinnies, and 7 bits can be taken away.

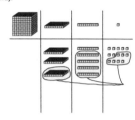

Addition and Subtraction   SG · Grade 4 · Unit 3 · Lesson 5   81

Student Guide - Page 81

Student Guide - Page 82

There are 2 flats, 1 skinny, and 7 bits left. Mrs. Haddad said she knew a different method to figure out how much candy is left.
This is what Mrs. Haddad did:

$$\begin{array}{r} 3\overset{5}{\cancel{6}}\overset{1}{\cancel{4}} \\ -\ 1\ 4\ 7 \\ \hline 2\ 1\ 7 \end{array}$$

4. Explain Mrs. Haddad's method in your own words.

Another day there were 1237 pieces of candy in the store. The store sold 459 pieces of candy that day. To find how much was left, Rhonda used Mrs. Haddad's method. Rhonda called this the **quick paper-and-pencil method for subtraction.**

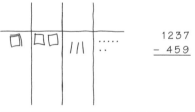

$$\begin{array}{r} 1237 \\ -\ 459 \end{array}$$

Joe saw that he had to trade 1 skinny for 10 bits to subtract 9 bits.

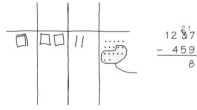

$$\begin{array}{r} 12\overset{2}{\cancel{3}}\overset{1}{7} \\ -\ 459 \\ \hline 8 \end{array}$$

82   SG · Grade 4 · Unit 3 · Lesson 5   Addition and Subtraction

Student Guide - Page 82

Discuss different ways of solving the problems. There are often easier methods than the standard algorithms. For example, the first problem, 501 – 199, can be solved by mental addition. A student may count up: 199-299-399-499 (that's 300) and 2 more makes 302. Another method is to start at 199 and move 1 forward to 200. Then from 200 to 500 we move 300. One more move forward takes us to 501 for a total number of 302 moves. Give students a chance to discover and discuss different methods of solving similar problems.

Ask students to estimate the answers to the following subtraction problems. They may use front-end estimation by thinking about the base-ten pieces or other convenient numbers.

$$659 - 78 \qquad 609 - 426$$
$$759 - 132 \qquad 4321 - 86 \qquad 2468 - 561$$

For example, for 659 – 78, students can think about 6 flats with 7 skinnies taken away. This leaves about 5 flats and 3 skinnies or about 530. After discussing students' estimates, ask students to compute the answers to the problems and compare their answers to the estimates. Encourage students to estimate answers whenever they are computing to help them recognize when their answers are not reasonable.

Read and discuss the Subtraction section in the *Student Guide. Questions 4–8* provide in-class practice. Students should then complete homework *Questions 11–19* in the *Student Guide.*

Student Guide - Page 83

Joe then broke up one flat so that he had 12 skinnies and was able to subtract.

$$\begin{array}{r} 12\overset{1}{\cancel{2}}\overset{1}{\cancel{3}}7 \\ -\ 459 \\ \hline 78 \end{array}$$

At the next step, Joe broke up his only pack so that he had 11 flats. Joe found that there were 778 pieces of candy left in the store.

$$\begin{array}{r} \overset{0}{\cancel{1}}\overset{1}{\cancel{2}}\overset{1}{\cancel{3}}7 \\ -\ 4\ 5\ 9 \\ \hline 7\ 7\ 8 \end{array}$$

For problems 5–8:

A. Use base-ten pieces or base-ten shorthand to solve the problem.
B. Then, do the problem using paper and pencil or mental math.

5. There were 578 pieces of candy in the store (5 flats, 7 skinnies, and 8 bits). The store sold 349 pieces of candy. How many pieces of candy were left?

6. Another day there were 4443 pieces of candy and 1718 of them were sold. How many pieces of candy were left?

7. There are 2075 Chocos. The store sold 1539. How many are left?

Addition and Subtraction   SG · Grade 4 · Unit 3 · Lesson 5   83

Student Guide - Page 83

Homework

In Questions 1 through 3, draw a picture of the problem using base-ten shorthand. Then, solve the problem using the picture to help you.

1. 364
   + 125

2. 1078
   + 2451

3. 1837
   + 2548

On Monday, Tuesday, and Wednesday, Rhonda and Joe were very busy and did not have time to compute their totals for the day. Help Rhonda and Joe compute their totals. Estimate to make sure your answer is reasonable.

Name	Monday	Tuesday	Wednesday
Rhonda	478	1003	576
Joe	589	1947	1756

4. How much candy was made on Monday?
5. How much candy was made on Tuesday?
6. Explain how you can compute the amount of candy made on Tuesday in your head.
7. How much candy was made on Wednesday?
8. How much candy did Rhonda make altogether on all three days?
9. How much candy did Joe make altogether on all three days?
10. How much candy did Rhonda and Joe make altogether on Monday, Tuesday, and Wednesday?

Solve the following problems. You may use any method you wish. Check your answer to make sure it is reasonable. Use base-ten shorthand when you need to.

11. 2357
    − 528

12. 2001
    − 432

13. 678
    + 1546

14. 1239
    − 643

Student Guide - Page 84

Unit 3: Home Practice

Part 1 Triangle Flash Cards: 5s and 10s
Study for the quiz on the multiplication facts for the fives and tens. Take home your *Triangle Flash Cards: 5s* and *10s* and your list of facts you need to study.

Here's how to use the flash cards. Ask a family member to choose one flash card at a time. He or she should cover the corner containing the highest number. This number will be the answer to a multiplication problem. Multiply the two uncovered numbers.

Study the math facts in small groups. Choose to study 8 to 10 facts each night. Your teacher will tell you when the quiz on the fives and tens will be.

Part 2 Addition and Subtraction
Use paper and pencil to solve the following problems.

1. 644
   + 53

2. 76
   + 29

3. 386
   − 21

4. 196
   − 77

5. 938
   − 449

6. 4015
   + 488

7. 5048
   − 274

8. 4653
   + 5664

Choose one problem. Be ready to explain how you can tell if the answer is reasonable.

Discovery Assignment Book - Page 23

---

15. The students from Livingston School and Stanley School are going on an outing. There are 765 students at Livingston School and 869 students at Stanley School. How many students are going on the outing?

16. To get free playground equipment, Livingston School needs to collect 4000 soup can labels by the end of the school year. In the first four months of school they collected 487 labels. By the end of the first semester they collected 752 more labels. How many more do they still need?

17. A high school has 2456 student desks. The principal decided that 548 of these desks should be replaced because they are not safe. How many old desks will be kept by the high school?

18. At Livingston School, Mr. Jones gave his class the following problem: Maya had 4006 stamps in her stamp collection. She sold 1658 of them. How many stamps does she have left? How would you solve this problem?

Maya thought about the base-ten pieces to solve Question 18.

John thought, "I can count up and do it in my head: 1658-2658-3658. That's 2000. Then 658-758-858-958. That's 300. Then 58-68-78-88-98 is 40. So far 2340. I have 8 more to go, so 2348 is the answer."

19. Think about John's method. Can you think of another way to do this problem? Describe your method.

Student Guide - Page 85

Part 3 People and Prices

1. Some of the workers at the TIMS Candy Company went to the fruit stand for lunch. Maggie bought a plum for 29¢ and an apple for 39¢. If she pays with $1.00, how much change should she receive?

2. A comic book at the used book sale costs 5¢. Special edition comic books cost 10¢ each. How much does Shannon need to pay if she wants to purchase 3 regular comic books and 4 special edition comic books?

3. Roberto's father is a salesman for the TIMS Candy Company. At the end of the year, Roberto's father earned a bonus of $565. This was $180 more than last year's bonus.
   A. How much did Roberto's father receive as a bonus last year?

   B. How can you be sure your answer is reasonable?

4. Ana went to the movies. She only had dimes with her. If the movie costs $1.75, how many dimes does she need to give the cashier? Explain.

5. Jessie went with her family to a two-day fall festival. On the first day, 4367 adults attended the fest and 4587 children attended.
   A. The newspaper reported the actual attendance. Calculate the actual attendance for the first day.

   B. About how many more people need to attend on the second day to reach a total of 10,000 people at the festival? Explain.

Discovery Assignment Book - Page 24

Daily Practice and Problems: Tasks for Lesson 5

H. Task: Fingers and Toes
(URG p. 16)

1. How many fingers are in the room right now? How many toes?

2. About how many fingers are in the school right now? About how many toes?

3. Explain how you solved Question 2.

4. There are 40 fingers around our table. How many hands are there? How many people?

J. Task: Take It Away! (URG p. 17)

Do these problems in your head.

1.	4003	2.	4007	3.	4001
	−3997		−3995		−3800

4.	4000	5.	4000	6.	4000
	− 500		− 501		− 499

7. Explain your strategies for Question 1 and Question 5.

L. Task: Working with Fact Families for × and ÷ (URG p. 18)

Solve the problems below and complete the number sentences for the related facts.

A. $5 \times 10 =$ __
   __ $\div 5 =$ __
   __ $\div 10 =$ __
   __ $\times 5 =$ __

B. $7 \times 5 =$ __
   __ $\div 7 =$ __
   __ $\div 5 =$ __
   __ $\times 7 =$ __

C. $3 \times 10 =$ __
   __ $\div 3 =$ __
   __ $\div 10 =$ __
   __ $\times 10 =$ __

D. $80 \div 8 =$ __
   __ $\times 8 =$ __
   $80 \div$ __ $=$ __
   $8 \times$ __ $=$ __

E. $20 \div 5 =$ __
   __ $\times 5 =$ __
   $5 \times$ __ $=$ __
   $20 \div$ __ $=$ __

F. $10 \times 9 =$ __
   __ $\div 9 =$ __
   __ $\div$ __ $= 9$
   $9 \times$ __ $=$ __

Suggestions for Teaching the Lesson

Math Facts

DPP items H, K, and L provide practice with multiplication and division with fives and tens.

Homework and Practice

- Assign the Homework section of the *Addition and Subtraction* Activity Pages in the *Student Guide.* Assign **Questions 1–10** after Part 1 of this activity. Assign **Questions 11–19** after Part 2 of this activity.

- For DPP Bits G and I, students play the *Digits Game,* providing practice in multidigit addition and subtraction computation and conceptualization.

- DPP Task J provides practice with mental subtraction.

- Assign Parts 2 and 3 of the Home Practice.

Answers for Parts 2 and 3 of the Home Practice can be found in the Answer Key at the end of this lesson and at the end of this unit.

Assessment

- Use the *Place Value Addition and Subtraction Quiz* Assessment Blackline Master to assess students' understanding and progress in skill development.

- Have students explain two different ways of solving the problem 201 − 74. Have them use base-ten pieces for one of the ways.

- Use the *Observational Assessment Record* to record students' progress in adding and subtracting multidigit numbers and in estimating reasonable solutions.

AT A GLANCE

Math Facts and Daily Practice and Problems

DPP items H, K, and L provide math facts practice. DPP items G and I provide practice adding and subtracting. Task J is an exercise in mental math.

Part 1. Addition with Base-Ten Pieces

1. As a class solve addition problems using base-ten pieces, *Base-Ten Board Parts 1* and *2*, and the *Recording Sheet.* Use the context of the TIMS Candy Company.
2. Alongside your work with the pieces, work the problems using the quick paper-and-pencil method for addition. Use the *Recording Sheet* to show your work.
3. Students practice addition with regrouping using the base-ten pieces and the quick paper-and-pencil method.
4. Discuss estimating by picturing the base-ten pieces.
5. Students read and discuss the Addition section of the *Addition and Subtraction* Activity Pages in the *Student Guide* and complete *Questions 1–3.*

Part 2. Subtraction with Base-Ten Pieces

1. As a class solve subtraction problems using base-ten pieces and *Base-Ten Board Parts 1* and *2.* Using the context of the TIMS Candy Company, solve problems that involve no regrouping, one regrouping, and two regroupings.
2. Alongside your work with the pieces, work the problems using the quick paper-and-pencil method for subtraction.
3. Students practice subtraction with regrouping using the pieces and the quick paper-and-pencil method.
4. Discuss how students can mentally compute subtraction problems. They also estimate the answers to subtraction problems.
5. Students read and discuss the Subtraction section of the *Addition and Subtraction* Activity Pages in the *Student Guide* and complete *Questions 4–8.*

Homework

1. Students complete *Questions 1–19* in the Homework section of the *Addition and Subtraction* Activity Pages in the *Student Guide.*
2. Students complete Parts 2 and 3 of the Home Practice.

Assessment

1. The *Place Value Addition and Subtraction Quiz* can be used as assessment.
2. Use the *Observational Assessment Record* to note students' abilities to add and subtract multidigit numbers and check the reasonableness of their answers.

Notes:

Place Value Addition and Subtraction Quiz

For each problem, estimate to be sure your answer is reasonable.

1.   435
     + 298

2. Explain a way to do Question 1 in your head.

3. Sketch 2782 using base-ten shorthand.

4.   2782
     – 1836

5.   5002
     – 476

6. Explain your estimation strategy for Question 5.

Student Guide

Questions 1–8 (SG pp. 79–84)

1.

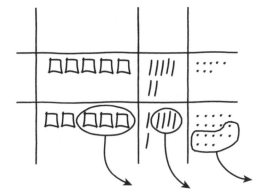

2. Answers will vary. Mrs. Haddad knew 6 + 8 + 7 = 21. She put down the 1 in the ones' place and wrote a little 2 in the tens' column to show 2 more tens. She added 4 tens + 7 tens + 6 tens + 2 tens and got 19 tens or 1 hundred and 9 tens. She put down the 9 in the tens' place and wrote a 1 above the hundreds' column. She added 8 hundreds + 7 hundreds + 1 hundred. She got 16 hundreds or 1 thousand and 6 hundreds. She put down the 6 in the hundreds' place and added 1 thousand and 1 thousand. She recorded a 2 in the thousands' place.

3. Answers will vary. Accept answers between 700–800.

4. Answers will vary. Mrs. Haddad traded 1 skinny for 10 bits, leaving 5 skinnies and 14 bits. She then subtracted 7 bits from 14 bits and wrote down 7 in the ones' place. She then subtracted 4 skinnies from 5 skinnies and wrote down 1 in the tens' place. Mrs. Haddad finally subtracted 1 flat from 3 flats. She wrote down a 2 in the hundreds' place.

5. A. 229 pieces of candy

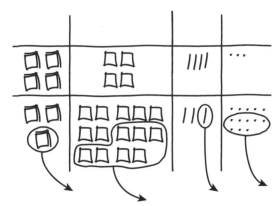

B.
$$\begin{array}{r} \overset{61}{5\cancel{7}8} \\ -\ 349 \\ \hline 229 \end{array}$$

6. A. 2725 pieces of candy

B.
$$\begin{array}{r} \overset{31}{4}\overset{31}{4}\cancel{4}3 \\ -\ 1718 \\ \hline 2725 \end{array}$$

*Answers and/or discussion are included in the Lesson Guide.

**Answers for all the Home Practice in the *Discovery Assignment Book* are at the end of the unit.

URG • Grade 4 • Unit 3 • Lesson 5 • Answer Key 73

7. A. 536 chocos are left.

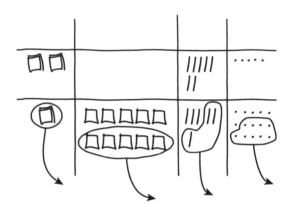

B.
```
   11 61
  2̶0̶7̶5̶
- 1539
  ────
   536
```

8. A. No, only 4639 chocos are left.

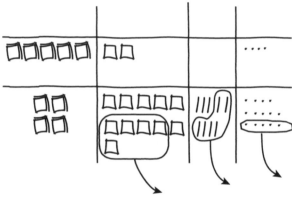

B.
```
   4 1 91
  5̶2̶0̶4̶
-  565
  ────
  4639
```

Homework (SG pp. 84–85)

Questions 1–19

1. 489

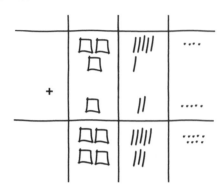

2. 3529

3. 4385

---

*Answers and/or discussion are included in the Lesson Guide.

**Answers for all the Home Practice in the *Discovery Assignment Book* are at the end of the unit.

74 URG • Grade 4 • Unit 3 • Lesson 5 • Answer Key

4. Estimates will vary—more than 1000.
   1067 pieces

5. Estimates will vary—about 3000. 2950 pieces

6. Answers will vary. Students might add three to
   47 to make 50. Then, they can add 1000 and
   1900 to get 2900. 2900 + 50 = 2950.

7. Estimates will vary—1800 + 600 = 2400.
   2332 pieces

8. Estimates will vary—about 2100. 2057 pieces

9. Estimates will vary—about 4200. 4292 pieces

10. Estimates will vary—more than 6000.
    6349 pieces

11. 1829

12. 1569

13. 2224

14. 596

15. 1634 students

16. 2761 labels

17. 1908 desks

18. 2348 stamps; Strategies will vary. Students can
    use base-ten pieces or paper and pencil to
    solve the problem.

19. Methods will vary. One possible method is to
    first subtract 1000 from 4006 to get 3006.
    Then, subtract 600 from 3006 to get 2406.
    Then, subtract 50 to get 2356. Finally, subtract
    8 to get 2348.

Discovery Assignment Book

**Home Practice (DAB pp. 23–24)

Part 2. Addition and Subtraction

Questions 1–8

1. 697

2. 105

3. 365

4. 119

5. 489

6. 4503

7. 4774

8. 10,317

Part 3. People and Prices

Questions 1–5

1. 32¢

2. 55¢

3. A. $385.00

   B. Answers will vary. Students could
   use convenient numbers such as
   560 − 200 = 360.

4. 18 dimes

5. A. 8954 people

   B. Estimates will vary. Accept between
   1000–2000 people. Possible strategy:
   10,000 − 9000 = 1000.

Unit Resource Guide

Place Value Addition and Subtraction Quiz (URG p. 72)

Questions 1–6

1. 733

2. Answers will vary. Students could add 2 to 298
   to make it 300. They could then add 300 to 435
   to get 735. They must then subtract 2 to get 733.

3. 🁣🁣 🁢🁢🁢🁢🁢🁢🁢 ||||/||| ··

4. 946

5. 4526

6. Possible strategy: 5000 − 500 = 4500.

---

*Answers and/or discussion are included in the Lesson Guide.

**Answers for all the Home Practice in the *Discovery Assignment Book* are at the end of the unit.

OPTIONAL LESSON

There are no Daily Practice and Problems items for this lesson.

What's Below Zero?

Estimated Class Sessions: 1

Students explore negative numbers in a variety of contexts and use calculators and number lines to solve problems.

Key Content

* Exploring negative numbers.
* Representing positive and negative integers on a number line.

Key Vocabulary

negative number
positive number

Curriculum Sequence

Before This Unit

Negative Numbers. This is the introduction to negative numbers in the *Math Trailblazers* curriculum. Students represented multiplication on number lines in Unit 7 of Grade 3.

After This Unit

Negative Numbers. In Grade 5 Unit 10, students will explore negative numbers in four-quadrant graphs.

Materials List

		Optional Activity	Homework	Written Assessment
Student Books	**Student Guide**	*What's Below Zero?* Pages 86–90 Page 91	*What's Below Zero?* Homework Section	
	Discovery Assignment Book	*Number Line* Page 35		
Teacher Resource	**Unit Resource Guide**			*Professor Peabody Made a Mess!* Page 83, 1 per student

⊙ *available on Teacher Resource CD*

All Transparency Masters, Blackline Masters, and Assessment Blackline Masters in the Unit Resource Guide are on the Teacher Resource CD.

Supplies for Each Student

scissors
glue or tape
calculator

Materials for the Teacher

large classroom number line, optional
classroom weather thermometer, optional

Student Guide - Page 86

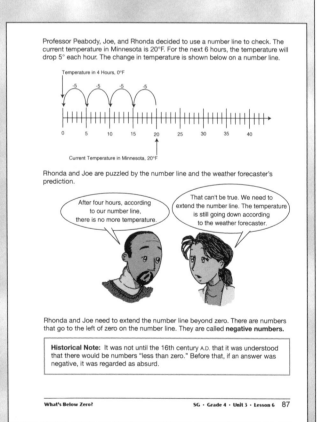

Student Guide - Page 87

Before the Activity

Before beginning this activity discuss temperature and temperature change with students. Watch the news the evening before and record the high and low temperature. Then, give students the low temperature and the change in temperature and have them find the high temperature.

Review DPP item K dealing with skip counting by fives and tens on a calculator with positive numbers. Have students complete this DPP item before beginning the activity to review skip counting with positive numbers. In this activity, students will skip count with negative numbers to solve problems.

> **TIMS Tip**
>
> Make sure that the calculators used for this activity will display negative numbers.

Developing the Activity

Instruct students to read the first page of the *What's Below Zero?* Activity Pages in the *Student Guide* for an introduction to negative numbers. Here, Professor Peabody, Joe, and Rhonda travel to another state and want to know what the temperature will be when they arrive.

Ask students how they might find out what temperature it will be in Minnesota in six hours if the current temperature is 20 degrees and the temperature drops five degrees per hour. Students might suggest skip counting backwards, subtracting five six times, using a calculator, or using a thermometer. All are good suggestions, and you may want to solve the problem using a few of the suggestions.

Show students how they can solve the problem using a number line. Display a large classroom number line on the chalkboard or simply draw one with only positive numbers. Ask students where 20 degrees is on the number line. Point to the number 20. Then, ask students how they might find out what temperature it will be in only 1 hour. Students should suggest moving five degrees to the left on the number line. Make a five degree hop to the left along the number line to show what the temperature will be in one hour. (15 degrees) Illustrate the temperature change for the next 3 hours until you reach 0 degrees. See Figure 21. Then, ask students what the temperature will be in another two hours. Some students may be confused as the number line ends at zero while others may already be familiar with thermometers and temperatures below zero.

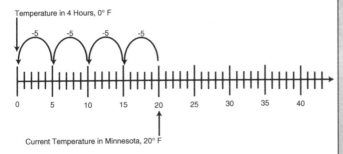

Figure 21: *Using a number line to skip count backwards*

Tell students that there are numbers that are to the left of zero on the number line. These numbers are called **negative numbers.** Numbers that are to the left of zero on the number line are called negative numbers while numbers that are on the right of zero on the number line are called **positive numbers.** (In this activity, we often refer to numbers that are to the "left of zero" as "below zero" since we are referring to thermometers and temperature.) Extend the number line to the left of zero to show negative numbers and solve the problem.

TIMS Tip

In order to avoid confusion with changes in temperature and with adding or subtracting negative numbers, discuss changes in temperature using the terms: rise and drop.

Have students cut out and assemble the number line on the *Number Line* Activity Page in the *Discovery Assignment Book.* Students can then model the problem on their own number lines. Encourage students to read about how Joe and Rhonda solved the problem on the *What's Below Zero?* Activity Pages.

TIMS Tip

Students who are familiar with temperatures that are below zero may live in areas that have cold winters. Encourage students to tell about times when the temperature was below zero. Illustrate why we say the temperature is "below zero" with a thermometer.

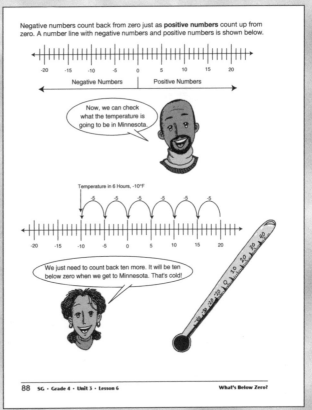

Student Guide - Page 88

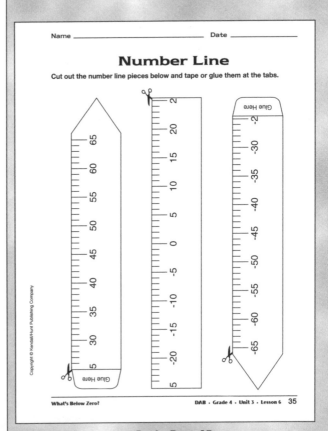

Discovery Assignment Book - Page 35

I must have forgotten my negative sign earlier when I said that the temperature would be 10°F.

It's a good thing we checked!

You can tell the difference between negative and positive numbers by the way they are written. "Negative five" is written as "-5."

1. Check Joe and Rhonda's calculations for the temperature when they arrive in Minnesota with your calculator. Skip count backwards by subtracting 5. Start at 20 and press ⊟ 5 six times.

2. Describe what happened in your calculator's window as you subtracted five, six times.

Your calculator should show that the temperature in Minnesota in six hours will be -10°.

Joe, Rhonda, and Professor Peabody arrive in Minnesota and find that the temperature is in fact -10°F. They watch the weather report and find that the temperature will be twenty degrees warmer on Monday morning.

3. A. Use your number line to find the temperature on Monday morning if the current temperature is -10°F.
   B. Use your calculator to verify your work on the number line.

Student Guide - Page 89

Joe, Rhonda, and Professor Peabody stay in Minnesota for a week. Professor Peabody recorded the temperature each morning and the change in temperature throughout the day.

This is shown in the data table below:

Day of Week	Temperature in Morning	Change in Temperature	Temperature in Evening
Monday	10°	drops 15°	
Tuesday	-5°	rises 35°	
Wednesday	-20°	drops 10°	
Thursday	15°	rises 20°	
Friday	20°	drops 20°	

4. Tell the temperature in the evening for each day. Use your number line and check your answer with a calculator.

5. On Friday evening, Joe, Rhonda, and Professor Peabody return to Arizona and find that the temperature is 85°F. If the temperature was -5°F when they left Minnesota, what is the change in temperature from Minnesota to Arizona? Explain.

Student Guide - Page 90

Continue to solve Joe and Rhonda's problem illustrating other ideas that students may have had. For example, to solve Joe and Rhonda's problem on a calculator, students could enter 20 − 5 − 5 − 5 − 5 − 5 − 5 = .
Students might also enter 20 − 30 = since $6 \times 5 = 30$. Encourage students to tell what they see in their calculator windows as they subtract five repeatedly. They should notice that a negative sign appears before the solution.

Many calculators have a "change sign" key (+C−). Have students take a moment to explore this key. Students can enter a positive number into the calculator, press +C− and see what happens.

The +C− key changes a positive number to a negative number. If students press the key again, the negative number will then change to a positive. If a temperature was negative to start with and then it got warmer, students could use the +C− key to enter the negative number into the calculator and add on the change in temperature.

Encourage students to verify Joe and Rhonda's calculations for the temperature on their arrival in Minnesota in **Question 1**. Students will describe how a negative number is shown on their calculator in **Question 2**.

In **Question 3**, students use their number line to find the temperature on Monday morning. After finding the answer, they should use calculators to get the same answer. Students will start on a negative number and add. A positive number will result.

Question 4 asks students to complete a table with a variety of calculations using negative and positive numbers. Students should complete the table using both the number line and their calculators for each calculation. They can work in pairs with one student using the calculator and one student using the number line, comparing answers and then trading tasks. Encourage students to skip count when using the number line. For example, when the temperature starts at 10° and drops 15°, students count backwards: 10°, 5°, 0°, -5°.

Using the calculator, the students have to enter a negative number first to complete two of the rows in the data table (Tuesday and Wednesday). They may need assistance with these rows. Possible keystrokes for these rows are: 5 +C− + 35 = and 20 +C− − 10 = .

Students may be tempted to use the calculator exclusively. However, repeated work with the number line is essential in order for students to develop a solid conceptual understanding of the relationships between positive and negative numbers. Use of the calculator, although an essential skill itself, does not provide the same visualization.

In *Question 5* students must tell the amount of change between two temperatures. Encourage students to place a marker on their number line at the starting and the ending temperature and to count the interval in between.

Suggestions for Teaching the Lesson

Homework and Practice

Assign the problems in the Homework section of the *What's Below Zero?* Activity Pages. Students will encounter negative numbers in a variety of contexts. If students are unfamiliar with altitudes below sea level or negative balances in a bank account, you might want to discuss these instances where negative numbers may be found.

Assessment

Use the *Professor Peabody Made a Mess!* Assessment Blackline Master to see if your students can use number lines, calculators, or other methods to solve problems involving negative numbers.

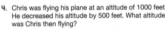

Homework

Temperature Time
Use your number line or a calculator to find the final temperature for each of the temperature changes below.

1. It was -30°F at 10:00 this morning. The high temperature for the day was 10° higher than the temperature at 10:00 this morning. What was the high temperature for the day?

2. It was 20°F at 8:00 last night. The temperature dropped 20° overnight to reach the day's low temperature. What was the low temperature for the day?

3. The weather forecaster said that the current temperature is -15°F. The temperature is expected to drop 10 more degrees to reach the low temperature for the day. What is the low temperature expected to be?

Flying
Use a calculator to solve each of the following problems. List the keystrokes you used to solve each problem.

4. Chris was flying his plane at an altitude of 1000 feet. He decreased his altitude by 500 feet. What altitude was Chris then flying?

5. Walt took off from an airport whose altitude is 100 feet below sea level. He then flew his plane 600 feet up. What altitude was Walt then flying?

At the Bank
Show your work as you solve each of the following problems.

6. Sean opened a savings account with $50.00. He withdrew $45.00 and put it into a checking account. How much money was left in Sean's savings account?

7. Cindy opened a checking account with $5.00. She then wrote a check for $10.00. What is the balance in Cindy's account?

What's Below Zero?   SG · Grade 4 · Unit 3 · Lesson 6   91

Student Guide - Page 91

Developing the Activity

1. Students read the first page of the *What's Below Zero?* Activity Pages in the *Student Guide*.

2. Students discuss how they might solve Professor Peabody, Joe, and Rhonda's dilemma.

3. Students are introduced to numbers below zero on the number line.

4. Students cut out and assemble number lines from the *Number Line* Activity Page in the *Discovery Assignment Book*.

5. Students read how Joe and Rhonda solved their temperature problem on the *What's Below Zero?* Activity Pages.

6. Students use their number lines and calculators to find the temperature in Minnesota.

7. Students explore the change sign key on their calculators.

8. Students solve *Questions 1–5* using their calculators and number lines.

Homework

Assign the Homework section on the *What's Below Zero?* Activity Pages.

Assessment

Students complete the *Professor Peabody Made a Mess!* Assessment Blackline Master.

Notes:

Professor Peabody Made a Mess!

Professor Peabody spilled coffee on the morning paper. His coffee stained parts of the weather section of the paper. Help Rhonda and Joe find out what the stained parts of the paper say. You may use your number line.

25¢

Minnesota State Daily Weather

Temperatures all over Minnesota have seen record changes this past week!

Day of Week	Temperature in Morning	Change in Temperature	Temperature in Evening
Monday	40°	drops 55°	■
Tuesday	-35°	■	15°
Wednesday	■	drops 70°	-10°
Thursday	45°	rises 20°	■
Friday	-10°	■	-30°

1. Monday _____   2. Tuesday _____

3. Wednesday _____   4. Thursday _____

5. Friday _____

6. Explain how you solved Question 2.

Student Guide

Questions 1–5 (SG pp. 89–90)

1. Joe and Rhonda were correct.

2. Answers will vary. One possible response is that the numbers changed from positive to negative.

3. *The temperature on Monday morning will be 10°F. For *Question 3A* students start on -10 on the number line. Since the temperature rises 20 degrees, students move to the right 20 on the number line. For *Question 3B,* students might use the following expression on their calculators: -10 + 20 =.

4. *

Day of Week	Temperature in Evening
Monday	-5°
Tuesday	30°
Wednesday	-30°
Thursday	35°
Friday	0°

5. 90°

Homework (SG p. 91)

Questions 1–7

1. -20°F
2. 0°F
3. -25°F
4. 500 feet
5. 500 feet
6. $5.00
7. -$5.00

Unit Resource Guide

Professor Peabody Made a Mess! (URG p. 83)

Questions 1–6

1. -15°
2. rises 50°
3. 60°
4. 65°
5. drops 20°
6. Possible strategy: There is a rise of 35° from -35° to 0° and another rise of 15° from 0° to 15°. 35 + 15 = 50°.

*Answers and/or discussion are included in the Lesson Guide.

**Answers for all the Home Practice in the *Discovery Assignment Book* are at the end of the unit.

LESSON GUIDE

At the Hardware Store

Estimated Class Sessions: 1–2

Students work a series of addition and subtraction word problems. The problems contain multidigit numbers and call for a variety of strategies: paper and pencil, estimation, and mental math.

Key Content

- Adding and subtracting using paper and pencil.
- Solving problems involving addition and subtraction.
- Choosing to find an estimate or an exact answer.
- Estimating sums and differences.
- Solving multistep word problems.
- Communicating solutions orally and in writing.
- Connecting mathematics with real-life situations.
- Choosing appropriate methods and tools to calculate (calculator, paper and pencil, or mental math).

Daily Practice and Problems: Bit for Lesson 7

M. Quiz on 5s and 10s (URG p. 19)

A. $5 \times 2 =$ B. $3 \times 10 =$ C. $5 \times 5 =$

D. $8 \times 10 =$ E. $6 \times 10 =$ F. $5 \times 3 =$

G. $10 \times 9 =$ H. $7 \times 5 =$ I. $10 \times 2 =$

J. $10 \times 7 =$ K. $6 \times 5 =$ L. $5 \times 10 =$

M. $8 \times 5 =$ N. $9 \times 5 =$ O. $4 \times 10 =$

P. $4 \times 5 =$ Q. $10 \times 10 =$

DPP Challenge is on page 89. Suggestions for using the DPPs are on pages 89–90.

Curriculum Sequence

Before This Unit

Students have solved word problems throughout their experiences with *Math Trailblazers*. Students completed sets of word problems in Grade 4 Unit 1 Lesson 6 in the *Student Guide* and the Home Practice in Units 1 and 2 in the *Discovery Assignment Book*.

After This Unit

Students will continue to encounter sets of word problems throughout fourth grade. For examples, see Unit 5 Lesson 7 and Unit 7 Lesson 8 in the *Student Guide*. See also the Home Practice for Units 4, 7, 8, 10, 13, 14, and 15 in the *Discovery Assignment Book*.

Materials List

Print Materials for Students

	Math Facts and Daily Practice and Problems	Activity	Homework	Written Assessment
Student Books — Student Guide		*At the Hardware Store* Pages 92–93		
Student Books — Discovery Assignment Book			Home Practice Part 6 Page 27	Home Practice Part 7 Page 28
Teacher Resources — Facts Resource Guide	DPP Item 3M			DPP Item 3M *Quiz on 5s and 10s*
Teacher Resources — Unit Resource Guide	DPP Items M–N Page 19			DPP Item M *Quiz on 5s and 10s* Page 19

available on Teacher Resource CD

All Transparency Masters, Blackline Masters, and Assessment Blackline Masters in the Unit Resource Guide are on the Teacher Resource CD.

Materials for the Teacher

Observational Assessment Record (Unit Resource Guide, Pages 9–10 and Teacher Resource CD)
Individual Assessment Record Sheet (Teacher Implementation Guide, Assessment section and Teacher Resource CD)

Developing the Activity

This set of problems addresses specific skills that are featured in this unit, namely addition and subtraction of multidigit numbers. Students must understand the structure of the problem and then employ the correct addition and subtraction computations to solve it. For further information about problem sets, see the TIMS Tutor: *Word Problems* in the *Teacher Implementation Guide.*

This set of problems serves two primary purposes. The first is to give increased practice in adding and subtracting multidigit numbers in the context of word problems. The second purpose is to develop students' estimation skills.

Using the Problems. Students can work on the problems individually, in pairs, or in groups. One approach is to ask students to work on the problems individually at first and then to come together in pairs or small groups to compare solutions. Then the group's solutions can be shared with others in a class discussion. The problems can also be assigned for homework. Because this activity does not require much teacher preparation, it is appropriate to leave for a substitute teacher.

Many problems such as those in *Questions 1* and *2* are straightforward computation problems. Encourage students to do a quick mental estimate prior to the computations, even when the problem does not specifically ask for an estimate. They can then check both their estimation and computation skills.

Question 4 asks students to think of a way to subtract 1005 from 2675 mentally. One possible strategy is to subtract 1000 to get 1675 and then to subtract 5 to get 1670.

Question 6 requires the students to first convert quarts to gallons before computing. This is a good time to remind students that before adding or subtracting quantities, they must check to make sure the quantities are given in the same units. Have a gallon measure and a quart measure available so that students can see that it does not make sense just to add the numbers without converting the measuring unit. Ask students to describe their strategies for converting quarts into gallons (240 qts ÷ 4 = 60 gal).

Questions 8, 9, and *11* are multistep problems in which students must read the problems carefully. *Question 8* requires students to recognize that the gardener bought 2 large bags of seed and that therefore the square footage of a large bag must be added twice before adding the square footage of the small bag. Students should also recognize that an estimate is all that is needed.

 At the Hardware Store

Answer the following questions about the hardware store. Make sure you estimate to check if your answer is reasonable.

1. The hardware store has 576 drywall nails and 852 wood nails. How many drywall and wood nails does the store have altogether?

2. The hardware store has 217 cans of varnish. The store sold 89. How many are left?

3. The hardware store sells seed packets. It has 1145 vegetable seed packets and 2356 flower seed packets.
   A. Estimate the total number of seed packets in the store.
   B. Find the exact number of seed packets in the store.

4. On Monday morning the hardware store had 2675 flower seed packets. By Friday, 1005 of these packets had sold.
   A. How many flower seed packets were left?
   B. Explain a way to do this problem in your head.

5. The hardware store has 672 gallon cans of white indoor paint and 743 gallon cans of white outdoor paint. How many cans of white paint does the store have altogether?

92   SG · Grade 4 · Unit 3 · Lesson 7   At the Hardware Store

Student Guide - Page 92

Student Guide - Page 93

Large Bags	Small Bags	Total sq ft	Excess in sq ft	Cost
4	0	13,100	2,100	$20.00
3	1	11,595	595	17.50
2	2	10,090	Short 910	15.00
2	3	11,860	860	17.50
1	4	10,355	Short 645	15.00
1	5	12,125	1,125	17.50
0	6	10,620	Short 380	15.00
0	7	12,390	1,390	17.50

Figure 22: *Buying sacks of grass seed*

Question 9 builds on the information in *Question 8.* In *Question 9,* students are given the total number of square yards and must determine how many of each size bag are needed to cover a lawn. There are several important mathematical considerations in this problem. One is that in some mathematics problems there may be more than one correct solution and nonmathematical considerations may come into play in choosing which is best. Have the students work at the problem before discussing it. Using a calculator or estimating possible solutions are appropriate strategies. Then ask different students to share their answers and rationales. Ask:

- *What if you went to the hardware store and told the shopkeeper that you only need to seed 800 sq ft? Can you buy $\frac{1}{2}$ bag of seed?* (Usually not, you must buy the whole bag because most shopkeepers will not want to split bags.)

- *Can you expect to be able to purchase the exact amount of grass seed you need for the 11,000 square feet?* (rarely)

- *If not, what will you do, buy slightly over or slightly under?* (Slightly over to make sure you have enough)

- *Can you think of some other products that come in packages that cannot be split?* (Some possible answers include paint, bread, paper clips, and potato chips.)

Given the constraints of the bag sizes available, there are several ways in which enough grass seed to seed the 11,000 square feet can be purchased. Some students may have chosen to "buy" only large sacks, some only small sacks and some a combination of the two. Any one of these approaches could give enough grass seed to cover the 11,000 square feet. Explore with the students which approach may be most efficient, cost effective, and least wasteful, and why. The different combinations of large and small bags can be compared by building a table. Start by filling in the data for four large bags and have the students fill in the rest of the table. Different groups can be responsible for different possibilities and then record their results on the class table. See Figure 22.

Ask:

- *Which combinations will give enough grass seed to seed the 11,000 square feet?* (4 large; 3 large, 1 small; 2 large, 3 small; 1 large, 5 small; 7 small)

- *Which will not?* (2 large, 2 small; 1 large, 4 small; 6 small)

- *Which will cost the most?* (4 large) *The least?* (2 large, 2 small; 1 large, 4 small; 6 small)

- *Which result in the least amount of extra grass seed?* (3 large, 1 small) *The most?* (4 large)

- *What do you recommend as the best way to buy the seed?*

- *What other factors might be considered in deciding whether to buy large or small bags?* (Here students may discuss such things as weight of the bags or the difficulty of carrying the large bags.)

Questions 10 and *11* require students both to add and subtract at different points in the solution path and to be able to determine which operations are appropriate.

Suggestions for Teaching the Lesson

Homework and Practice

- Assign some of the problems in this lesson for homework.

- Assign Part 6 of the Home Practice for homework. Part 6 provides a review of the geometry covered in Unit 2.

- DPP Challenge N presents an area and perimeter problem.

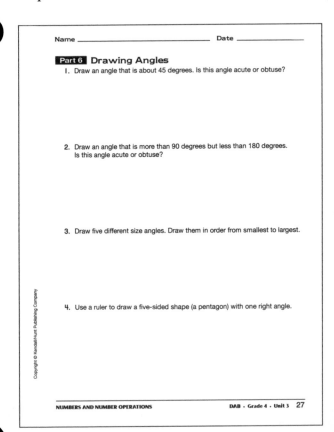

Daily Practice and Problems: Challenge for Lesson 7

N. Challenge: Antopolis Airport
  (URG p. 19)

Below is a sketch of the hangar at Antopolis Airport. (Planes are stored and repaired in hangars.)

Find the area and perimeter of the hangar. You may wish to build the hangar with square-inch tiles.

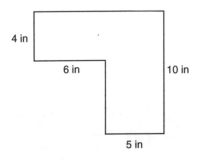

Name _____ Date _____

Part 7 Arithmetic Review
Use paper and pencil or mental math to solve these problems. Remember to do a quick estimate first and then look at your answer to make sure it makes sense.

1. 123 + 537	2. 672 − 253	3. 303 + 497
4. 897 + 481	5. 460 − 255	6. 461 791 + 23

7. Explain how you solved Question 3.

8. Explain how you can solve Question 4 using base-ten shorthand.

9. Explain your estimation strategy for Question 6.

28   DAB · Grade 4 · Unit 3   NUMBERS AND NUMBER OPERATIONS

Assessment

- Use Part 7 of the Home Practice as an assessment of paper-and-pencil addition and subtraction and of estimation.
- DPP Bit M is a quiz on the fives and tens multiplication facts.
- Use the *Observational Assessment Record* to note students' progress in computing multidigit addition and subtraction problems. Transfer appropriate documentation from the Unit 3 *Observational Assessment Record* to students' *Individual Assessment Record Sheets*.

AT A GLANCE

Math Facts and Daily Practice and Problems

DPP Bit M provides a quiz on the fives and tens multiplication facts. DPP Challenge N is a review of area and perimeter.

Developing the Activity

1. Students solve problems in *Questions 1–11* on the *At the Hardware Store* Activity Pages in the *Student Guide*.
2. Students discuss solutions and solution paths.

Homework

Assign Home Practice Part 6.

Assessment

1. DPP Bit M assesses the fives and tens multiplication facts.
2. Use Home Practice Part 7 as an assessment.
3. Use the *Observational Assessment Record* to record students' abilities to compute multidigit addition and subtraction problems.
4. Transfer appropriate documentation from the Unit 3 *Observational Assessment Record* to the *Individual Assessment Record Sheets*.

Notes:

Student Guide

Questions 1–11 (SG pp. 92–93)

1. 1428 nails

2. 128 cans

3. **A.** Answers will vary. Accept answers between 3000–4000 seed packets.

   B. 3501 seed packets

4.* **A.** 1670 seed packets

   B. Answers will vary. Students might take the five from 1005 and subtract it from 2675 to get 2670. They can then subtract the 1000 to get 1670.

5. 1415 cans of paint

6.* **A.** 60 gallons

   B. 320 gallons

7. 1810 feet

8.* Answers will vary. Accept answers between 8000–9000 square feet.

9.* **A.–B.** Answers will vary depending upon how many bags of each kind of seed the student chooses to buy. One possible solution is to buy 3 large bags and 1 small bag. The total cost would be $17.50.

10. **A.** Answers will vary. Students might want to use convenient or close numbers, or they might want to use front-end estimation.

    B. 848 pennies

    C. $8.48

    D. $1.03

11.* **A.** 118 bags

    B. 315 bags

    C. Over the weekend

    D. 79 bags

Discovery Assignment Book

**Home Practice (DAB pp. 27–28)

Part 6. Drawing Angles

Questions 1–4

1.–2. Students should not use protractors to draw these angles. They should use the benchmarks of 90 degrees and 180 degrees to help them draw the angles for *Questions 1* and *2*. The angle in *Question 1* is acute. The angle in *Question 2* is obtuse.

3. Drawings will vary.

4. Drawings will vary. Here is one possible solution.

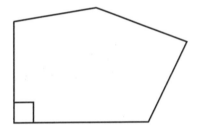

*Answers and/or discussion are included in the Lesson Guide.
**Answers for all the Home Practice in the *Discovery Assignment Book* are at the end of the unit.

URG • Grade 4 • Unit 3 • Lesson 7 • Answer Key   91

Part 7. Arithmetic Review

Questions 1–9

1. 660
2. 419
3. 800
4. 1378
5. 205
6. 1275
7. Strategies will vary. One possible solution that uses mental math: Take 3 away from 303 to make 300. Add it to 497 to make 500. $300 + 500 = 800$.

8.

🔲	—	.
8	9	7
4	8	1
12¹	1̶7̶	8
13	7	8

9. Strategies will vary. Possible strategy: $500 + 800 + 25 = 1325$.

*Answers and/or discussion are included in the Lesson Guide.
**Answers for all the Home Practice in the *Discovery Assignment Book* are at the end of the unit.

Discovery Assignment Book

Part 2. Addition and Subtraction

Questions 1–8 (DAB p. 23)

1. 697
2. 105
3. 365
4. 119
5. 489
6. 4503
7. 4774
8. 10,317

Part 3. People and Prices

Questions 1–5 (DAB p. 24)

1. 32¢
2. 55¢
3. A. $385.00

   B. Answers will vary. Students could use convenient numbers such as $560 - 200 = 360$.
4. 18 dimes
5. A. 8954 people

   B. Estimates will vary. Accept between 1000–2000 people. Possible strategy: $10,000 - 9000 = 1000$.

Part 4. Fact Families

Questions A–E (DAB p. 25)

A. $30 \div 5 = 6, 5 \times 6 = 30,$
   $30 \div 6 = 5$

B. $9 \times 10 = 90, 10 \times 9 = 90,$
   $90 \div 9 = 10$

C. $3 \times 5 = 15, 15 \div 3 = 5,$
   $5 \times 3 = 15$

D. $9 \times 5 = 45, 45 \div 5 = 9,$
   $45 \div 9 = 5$

E. $10 \times 5 = 50, 50 \div 5 = 10,$
   $50 \div 10 = 5$

Part 5. More Fact Families

Questions A–F (DAB p. 26)

A. $10 \times 10 = 100$
   $1000 \div 10 = 10$

B. $10 \div 5 = 2$
   $2 \times 5 = 10$
   $5 \times 2 = 10$
   $10 \div 2 = 5$

C. $30 \div 10 = 3$
   $30 \div 3 = 10$
   $3 \times 10 = 30$
   $10 \times 3 = 30$

D. $6 \times 5 = 30$
   $5 \times 6 = 30$
   $30 \div 6 = 5$
   $30 \div 5 = 6$

E. $7 \times 10 = 70$
   $10 \times 7 = 70$
   $70 \div 7 = 10$
   $70 \div 10 = 7$

F. $1 \times 5 = 5$
   $5 \times 1 = 5$
   $5 \div 5 = 1$
   $5 \div 1 = 5$

*Answers and/or discussion are included in the Lesson Guide.

Part 6. Drawing Angles

Questions 1–4 (DAB p. 27)

1–2. Students should not use protractors to draw these angles. They should use the benchmarks of 90 degrees and 180 degrees to help them draw the angles for *Questions 1* and *2*. The angle in *Question 1* is acute. The angle in *Question 2* is obtuse.

3. Drawings will vary.

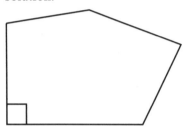

4. Drawings will vary. Here is one possible solution.

Part 7. Arithmetic Review

Questions 1–9 (DAB p. 28)

1. 660
2. 419
3. 800
4. 1378
5. 205
6. 1275
7. Strategies will vary. One possible solution that uses mental math: Take 3 away from 303 to make 300. Add it to 497 to make 500. $300 + 500 = 800$.

8.

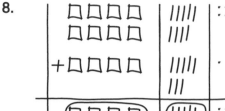

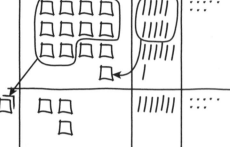

☐	—	•
8	9	7
4	8	1
12'	1̶7̶	8
13	7	8

9. Strategies will vary. Possible strategy: $500 + 800 + 25 = 1325$.

Answers and/or discussion are included in the Lesson Guide.